Parenting
from Your Soul

Parenting
from Your Soul

A Spiritual Approach to Raising Children
with Compassion and Wisdom

JEANMARIE WILSON

BALBOA
PRESS
A DIVISION OF H

Balboa Press books may be ordered through booksellers or by contacting:

Balboa Press
A Division of Hay House
1663 Liberty Drive
Bloomington, IN 47403
www.balboapress.com
1 (877) 407-4847

Because of the dynamic nature of the Internet, any web addresses or
links contained in this book may have changed since publication and
may no longer be valid. The views expressed in this work are solely those
of the author and do not necessarily reflect the views of the publisher,
and the publisher hereby disclaims any responsibility for them.

The author of this book does not dispense medical advice or prescribe the use
of any technique as a form of treatment for physical, emotional, or medical
problems without the advice of a physician, either directly or indirectly. The
intent of the author is only to offer information of a general nature to help
you in your quest for emotional and spiritual well-being. In the event you use
any of the information in this book for yourself, which is your constitutional
right, the author and the publisher assume no responsibility for your actions.

Any people depicted in stock imagery provided by Thinkstock are models,
and such images are being used for illustrative purposes only.
Certain stock imagery © Thinkstock.

Printed in the United States of America.

ISBN: 978-1-4525-9571-9 (sc)
ISBN: 978-1-4525-9572-6 (e)

Library of Congress Control Number: 2014906730

Balboa Press rev. date: 04/23/14

WITH LOVE TO my wonderful husband, Ron, who is always there to support me in every way.

Thank you to my beautiful daughters, Jessica and Samantha, who have taught me much about love, honesty, and forgiveness.

With much love to my mother, Camille, and my grandmother, Josephine, who have shown me what unconditional love truly is.

With appreciation to Michelle Thompson, a very talented writer and good friend, for her valuable insight and suggestions.

Thank you to the friends and family members who read the draft and offered support, advice, and encouragement.

With much gratitude to Beth Miller, whose guidance has been instrumental in the completion of this book and who has helped me on the journey to authentically embrace my creativity and self-expression.

Edited by Jessica Wilson, Artwork by Samantha Wilson

Copies of *Parenting from Your Soul* and reproductions of artwork by Samantha Wilson can be purchased at www. parentingfromyoursoul.com. You will find additional resources on parenting, self-growth, and healthy living at this site as well as new artwork by Samantha.

Thank you for your interest in *Parenting from Your Soul*!

Contents

Introduction

As I FACED an upcoming surgery for an illness that happened without much warning, I thought about what really mattered to me in my life, and it led me to consider my role as a parent. While I am proud of many decisions I have made, there are certainly things I would do differently, knowing what I know now. I wish I had picked up a book similar to this twenty years ago to help teach me to *parent from my soul.* In other words—how to love my children unconditionally, find patience in challenging times, practice forgiveness for myself and others, and radically accept my children throughout each stage of their growth.

There is nothing more important than the way we raise our children. All of our decisions have far-reaching consequences—for our children and for all those who come in contact with them, including their own children. The best choices, however, are not always clear at the time. Parenting, similar to self-growth, is a work-in-progress, minute-to-minute practice made up of gratifying experiences as well as ones that leave us wishing we had more insight and wisdom. Like you, I am striving to master my best self, as a parent and as an individual. With this book, you can practice spiritual concepts that will help you parent wisely and raise joyful, healthy children while creating more happiness in your own life.

I have worked as a school counselor for over twenty years and have been privileged to meet students and families who have taught me much about the human spirit, about honesty, compassion, and dedication, and prevailing over adversity. I have witnessed many exceptional examples of childrearing as well as some that were not so admirable. But in all of those moments, encompassing the magnificent and the misguided, the parent's love for their children was evident.

I wrote this book for a number of reasons but primarily because it is my hope that parents will benefit from my experience as a seasoned parent and school counselor and be inspired to view parenting choices through a new lens—one based in spiritual ideology. This outlook differs somewhat from traditional methods of parenting. It challenges us to look beyond the conventional approach of a parent-child relationship to one that contains a deeper level of clarity, insight, respect, and unconditional love. An outlook based in spirituality can help us:

- accept our children as they are, honoring their individual paths;
- recognize and appreciate the many phases of our children's growth;
- open our hearts to give and receive a deeper level of love;
- practice forgiveness for ourselves, our children, and others in our lives;
- encourage our children to live authentic lives filled with purpose and intention;
- show our children how to create the lives they want by claiming their power and understanding the universal laws of creation;
- make the changes we want in our lives by claiming our own power;
- transform our relationships with our children, no matter their ages, to relationships comprised of mutual acceptance, respect, compassion and honesty; and
- examine our day-to-day experiences with a greater level of awareness, acceptance, and meaning.

In order to facilitate a deeper level of communication and understanding within the parent-child relationship, I have added a section where parents (or other significant adults) can write their own heartfelt messages to their children. This may end up being the most important part of this book. You will also find many valuable resources about the concepts discussed in *Parenting from Your Soul* at the end.

Our world is in desperate need of emotionally healthy children who will have the confidence and resolve to contribute their gifts and talents to the world, making it a better place to reside, and as a result, leading their own children down a better path. It is essential that we improve the way we are raising our children, keeping what works and being open to changing what doesn't.

The principles I discuss will assist you to improve your relationship with your children, even if they are grown, as there is always potential for transformation. Have the courage to examine your outlook and consider another perspective. You may be surprised to discover a way to view parenting choices that you haven't considered.

Applying these principles will allow you to create more happiness for yourself and your children. After all, isn't that what life is really about?

Wishing you peace, harmony, and joy,

Jeanmarie

When you want to experience life and love on another level, you have a child.

A Parent's Love

Being deeply loved by someone gives you strength, while loving someone deeply gives you courage.

—Lao Tzu, ancient Chinese philosopher
and founder of Taoism

A PARENT'S LOVE is profound and pure; it infiltrates every cell of our bodies. It is magnificent, yet terrifying, to love so deeply. It is good that we do because there are many moments when our love is tested: when our sleep-deprived body hears the 3:00 a.m. cry of our infant, as we grit our teeth through our toddler's fourth tantrum of the day, as we anxiously await our teenager's arrival home past curfew, or when we grant acceptance to our adult child who does not make decisions we agree with. During those times—and many others—we will draw from this well of love.

This love has an intensity to it that can bring us to our knees and it changes our lives forever. We never look at the world again in the same way after we have children. Love for my children has pushed me to grow in ways that were sometimes painful, but which ultimately make me a better parent and a better person. I have often found myself in a place of raw vulnerability, a place that makes me more authentic and helps me realize what really matters.

Awareness stemming from this honest place helps me make choices that are better, not only for my children, but also for me. Because of this awareness, I have pushed myself to look authentically at my choices and my actions, my beliefs and my expectations, to see if they really serve me as a parent. Within this process, we may find things we don't like about ourselves. Those times are difficult, but looking at them honestly and objectively will only help us to evolve and grow.

Author Elizabeth Stone said, "Making the decision to have a child is momentous. It is to decide forever to have your heart go walking around outside your body." We become this vulnerable in order to experience the gifts that loving a child holds, but in order to do so, we have to let down our defenses and enter a place where we are real. It is a vulnerable place to reside, but it is the true essence of parenting.

Parenting, similar to aging, is not for the faint of heart. It is a sacred journey, filled with learning experiences for both parties, not all of which are easy. This journey requires that we are brave, honest, noble, and resilient. It contains challenges, but it is worth all of the difficulties we encounter. Love for our children carries us through this journey and encourages us to feel more, give more, and be more than we ever thought we were capable of.

When you want to experience life and love on another level, you have a child.

. . . .

This week, take a few moments to write down the gifts you have received by becoming a parent. How have you grown? What does being a parent really mean to you?

. . . .

Why We Do What We Do

When parents do too much for their children, the children will not do too much for themselves.

—Elbert Hubbard, American writer, publisher, artist, and philosopher

LET'S EXAMINE WHY we do what we do for our children. Do our actions come from a place of guilt? Are they directed by our egos and their need to control? Do we need to be needed just a little too much?

When we over-manage our children's lives, even from very early ages, we give our children the message that they are not capable. We don't let them learn how to navigate disappointment or fear. We teach them they don't have to be strong and resilient, that they can sit back because someone will come along to pick up the pieces for them. We do our children no favors by not setting boundaries or expecting a certain level of respect and behavior. Sometimes we do this because we want to give them more than we had or because we are trying to garner their love. It may stem from a feeling of remorse; we feel we were not enough at some point and are now overcompensating, but it never works. Almost all parents have been guilty of this to a degree, but we should spend some time reflecting on this form of parenting.

It is difficult to watch our children fall, and there is a strong desire to protect them from the disappointments of the world. Too much protection and manipulation, though, only makes things more difficult for our children when they get out into the world and we are not there to orchestrate events for them.

We need to let our children develop character, resiliency, and confidence by experiencing life and by living it—by feeling the difficult feelings that hurt us to see them go through. They need to face the consequences of making decisions for themselves and to learn about the power behind their choices. The only way they can learn this is through doing it.

I have seen parents enable their children and make excuses for them. I have seen parents doing their children's homework, choosing the colleges they apply to, and filling out their college applications. I have seen parents mortgage their homes and future financial security to pay exorbitant college tuition, bail their children out of jail, hire expensive lawyers, or send them for drug treatment time and time again. I have seen parents hover over their children's lives, making every decision for them. I have even seen them justify cruelty and cheating.

I understand the reason for it; there is fear in having to watch our children accept the consequences that stem from their choices. I understand that parents, often well-intentioned and caring individuals, experience difficulty when they have defined themselves by their children's accomplishments. Unfortunately, the cover-up and enabling of the present lead to bigger consequences in the future when the stakes are higher. It leads to children growing up to be adults who fall apart at the smallest amount of adversity. It leads to children who cannot make a decision for themselves, and it leads to laziness.

There is a fine line here. We can advocate for and protect our children, but we can't give them everything without letting them earn something. We need to let them grow, to help them see themselves as capable beings and to let them experience an environment where they can own the consequences of the decisions they make, both positive and negative. Sometimes, that includes what we might consider "failure."

When we come from a supportive place, we help when it is truly needed. We let our children know that we have faith in their

5

abilities and help them see that life includes making mistakes and learning from them. We encourage them to embrace the power that lies behind making choices. By looking at the big picture, we help our children develop tolerance, fortitude, and flexibility—all necessary attributes for independence and happiness.

Giving from a place of love, rather than fear, leads to children who grow up knowing they have all they need to be successful in the world.

. . . .

Consider a time when you did something for your children they could have done for themselves. How did this meet your needs? Would you make the same choice again?

. . . .

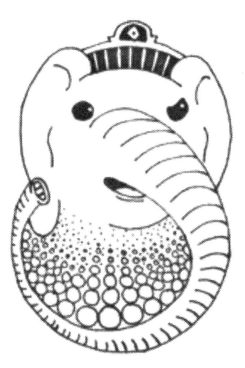

Why Being A Parent Makes Us So Crazy

No matter how calmly you try to referee, parenting will eventually produce bizarre behavior, and I'm not talking about the kids. Their behavior is always normal.

—Bill Cosby, American comedian, author, producer, educator, musician, and activist

LET'S FACE IT, parenting is a tough gig. The hours are long; the vacations nonexistent, and as far as positive feedback goes—not so much. There have been times when my childless friends have looked at me and smiled. It seemed as if they had it figured out a long time ago, just about when I was feeling sorry for them because of what they were missing. I would not trade my decision to become a parent for anything in the world, but there have been moments.

The reason this role makes us so crazy is because we know our mistakes can have serious consequences. We have watched as other parents made poor choices. We may have experienced firsthand how poor parenting affects a child and vowed to be different. We know our choices count.

It makes us crazy because we care so much. Careers come and go, relationships wax and wane, and our financial futures may be in jeopardy, but *nothing affects us like problems with our children; it reaches a part of us other experiences do not.* We say crazy things out of desperation, act in ways we do not recognize, and take action that makes little sense.

I recall a parent who submitted college applications for his son without his knowledge. I followed my twelve-year-old daughter and her friends on Halloween without telling them because I worried about their safety. My friend threw her sixteen-year-old son's belongings out on the lawn one day and changed the locks. I know another parent who assumed her daughter's identity on Facebook and disbanded a friendship she found unacceptable.

Eventually, it becomes too much. We act in crazy ways when things seem to be spiraling out of control (were we ever in control?), when we are losing our balance, and when we are reacting solely out of fear. We have to focus on doing our best and learning to let go because sound decisions are not made in a state of panic. We need to understand that we can't control everything, and we have to put some distance between the problem and ourselves. It is crucial to get objective feedback and to act from a loving place where we focus upon love for ourselves as much as for our children.

That is when you make decisions you can be proud of, even if they are not popular. This is where you can judge if your actions and words are self-serving or necessary.

This is the place where you may still act a little bit crazy, but where you are proud of what you do and say.

∙ ∙

Take a few minutes to recall a time when you overreacted out of fear. Consider how you could have handled the situation differently. What could you do if something like that came up again? What are some alternate strategies? How could you put some distance between the situation and your reaction?

∙ ∙

Teaching Our Children
About Service

Not all of us can do great things. But we can do small things with great love.

—Mother Teresa, Roman Catholic
religious sister and missionary

OUR SOCIETY CAN be self-centered, stemming from a fear that there is not enough of what we want and that what we have must be protected. We apply this to resources such as money, time, energy, and even love, but this belief is a fallacy since our universe is limitless. Teaching our children about the importance of not just taking from this source, but giving back, is vital; our goal should be to leave the world a better place simply because we were here.

While in hiding during the Holocaust, Anne Frank wrote, "How wonderful it is that nobody need wait a single moment before starting to improve the world." This does not mean we have to find a cure for a disease or win the Nobel Peace Prize. We are only asked to do our best and consider the plight of others in our travels.

Teaching our children about the importance of service to family, friends, community, and school will help them grow up to be vital, capable adults; making a contribution always helps children feel empowered. Service to others does not mean ignoring your own desires; conversely, your truest desires can be met simultaneously. This type of service means doing something that aligns with who you truly are. For example, it does not mean choosing to work in a profession that you dislike, but earns approval from your parents. Service to family might entail helping to care for a grandparent or getting a job as a teenager to help pay the bills when a parent has lost his or her job. It might mean standing up for a sibling who is getting teased in school. Service is doing something with a genuine heart and a clear purpose, one that not only matches your goals but also helps another at the same time.

This brings to mind a story of a tenth-grade student whose mother was diagnosed with a rare, debilitating disease. Her mother suddenly became bedridden and needed a lot of care. This young woman was a promising athlete, excellent student, and leader in her class. She made the decision to resign from her athletic teams, clubs, leadership roles, and other activities to come home every day after school to care for her mother. She removed all unnecessary activities from her day to help her family. She was there for her mother every day after school as well as on weekends, assisting with basic daily care and medical needs. Through all of this, she remained a stellar student. When we met for a college planning conference, she and her father were concerned about the lack of activities on her resume. I assured them that her contribution was much more valuable than any organized activity and would be looked upon very favorably; I am truly in awe of this young woman's sacrifice and service to her family.

We affect each other's lives for better or not. We can't avoid this as we are creating our lives in conjunction with others. All of our actions have far-reaching repercussions, more than we can ever imagine, and every action is either based in love or it isn't. Here, there is no gray area.

Service to others can include the traditional notion of volunteering your time, but it also includes the way you conduct your interactions with people on a daily basis. Making a contribution through a service-based career is honorable, but any undertaking that enriches the life of another can be viewed as a service; a comedian's contribution is no less noble than a preacher's. The important factor is how you perform this service and whether it is done with integrity, compassion, and respect.

I have seen many children today who lead their lives with a sense of entitlement, and it is not a pretty sight. It is a breakdown, not just on the part of the parents, but also of a society that encourages instant gratification and devalues attributes such as responsibility, independence, and accountability.

Demonstrate through your words, but more importantly through your actions, that we all have a responsibility to help other people, the creatures on our planet, and our environment.

Show your children that we have an obligation to make the world a better place just because we were here, and that when we do, it benefits them as much as it does others.

• •

Do something this week for someone in need of a kind word or gesture. How did this experience affect that person? How did it affect you?

• •

Denial

You can't get away from yourself by moving from one place to another.

—Ernest Hemingway, American author and journalist

FOR YEARS, WE joked that my mother was the "Queen of Denial." Although we laughed about it, her ability to ignore what she did not want to deal with could be frustrating. The house could fall down around her, and she would not even acknowledge it. The fact that she has dementia now, while difficult for her and our family, is a blessing in a way. I think it is my mother's way of coping with the challenges that aging has brought her, and I am grateful for the peace that denial now brings her.

Denial in parenting though, does not help us face situations that need attention. Instead, it prevents us from experiencing the uncomfortable feelings that precipitate change. Denial of our children's problems does not help our children in the way that they need however, denial can be sneaky and insidious. It fools us into believing what we want without even knowing it because denial works very hard to protect its dysfunction. Truly taking stock of a situation, being receptive to change, and accepting the truth of our experiences, however uncomfortable, helps break through that denial. If our children are in trouble and need direction or resources, pretending the problems don't exist only prolongs the inevitable and keeps a possible solution at bay, even if that solution is only acceptance for now.

I have witnessed instances of parents using denial to keep from confronting the issues their children were having: drugs, self-injury, eating disorders, cheating, suicidal thoughts, bullying, and so on. It has been frustrating as a school counselor to present direct evidence of a problem, only to have a parent minimize it and explain it away. But as a parent, I understand the insidiousness of denial because I have been there. It is different when the problem hits close to home; you can be blinded by what you do not want to face.

Be open to looking at your children's situations from a less-defended point of view when your children are struggling, when others point out an issue, or when things just don't feel right to you, and you may see areas that need attention.

At that point, you will be open to receiving the help you need to address those issues and support your children in the ways they need.

• •

Are there any areas of your children's lives that you could be in denial about? Is there an area that needs attention but is difficult to face? If so, give some thought to alternate ways of dealing with those situations. Get some objective advice, talk with trusted sources, seek out resources, and most importantly, be honest about your own feelings.

• •

We Create Our Own Experiences

Open your eyes, look within. Are you satisfied with the life you're living?

—Bob Marley, Jamaican singer-songwriter

OUR THOUGHTS, FEELINGS, and beliefs create our reality; the life we currently live is a result of what we embody and truly believe. It is the result of what we speak about, the emotions we react to, and what we ruminate over. If we embraced the notion that we could direct our thoughts and feelings, shift our energy, and learn to disregard the endless chatter in our heads, we would recognize the power we have. Our focus needs to embody the characteristics and feelings we would have if we were living the life we desired.

Motivational teacher, author, and founder of Hay House Publishing, Louise Hay noted, "Every thought we think and every word we speak are creating our own future. Our thoughts and our words go out into the universe, are accepted, and brought back to use as experience." Although this concept is simple, it requires that we take responsibility for our actions and what we focus our minds upon. It necessitates that we maintain awareness about how we start each day, how we embrace each day, and how we react to events in our days. For those of us who exclaim frustration over events in our lives we do not like, it give us a roadmap to create something different if we are willing to do the work. We are shown how to use the free will we were so graciously given to create a life of our choosing.

Because people are skeptical, undisciplined, or unmotivated, they end up getting blown around like leaves in the wind, wondering why their lives turned out as they have. This concept is powerful, and it is one I need to remind myself about often; it is easy to get distracted by the demands of my day. Louise Hay teaches us to use affirmations as a tool—positive statements that describe our intentions in the present tense. She shares that they are like planting seeds that cultivate our future experiences. Sprinkle these seeds with trust, faith, conviction, and strong intention. Add a healthy dose of gratitude, and create the life you want.

I was introduced to this concept several years ago, and coming from a place of feeling powerless over certain experiences, this possibility was like a brilliant flash of light to me. I wish I were able to impart this knowledge to my children when they were young so they would feel powerful in a world that considers children powerless; they would never again see themselves as victims. Imagine the influential creators our children would become, knowing they held the key to their happiness and life experiences and what this could do for our planet as a whole if people felt empowered and secure. Our world would radically change if people did not feel that what they wanted had to come from another. When we embody this concept, doors open that we thought were out of reach. As teacher and author Neale Donald Walsch so aptly put it, "You were created to create—not to react." There is power in recognizing that we create our lives with every thought we think, word we say, and choice we make.

There are times when I think I grasp the concept, but other times, I feel as though I have barely scratched the surface. However, I know my life is different because of this understanding. While my outer reality may be the same for now, I am not. I know there is power within all of us; it is our ability to create the lives we want by utilizing the free will we are all born with.

Because of this free will, we can choose to experience pain instead of happiness, sickness instead of wellness, and poverty instead of prosperity. When we look at it in those terms, it appears as though we are blaming people for their situations, but the opposite is true. It is not a matter of blame, but one of responsibility—the responsibility to remember a truth we have forgotten. Taking responsibility for our lives leads us to the realization that we are the ones in control of it. This awareness can change our lives in an instant when we realize that utilizing our free will is our greatest agent of change. Our belief in the difficulty of this concept creates an obstacle where there is none. As author Esther Hicks of Abraham-Hicks said, "It is as easy to create a castle as it is a button."

Imagine if we gave our children the knowledge that their lives originate where they focus their energy and attention because each moment contains the potential to transform the future. *Here is where the seeds of change begin!*

Too often, children grow up with the belief that the decisions they make are of little consequence. We have to empower our children to embrace the power of choice and teach them that nothing is more important than making choices that result in their happiness. We have to tell them that the words they choose to use and where they focus their thoughts and beliefs creates their lives. As it states in *A Course in Miracles*, a self-study program for personal transformation, every thought creates form on some level. Why don't we focus our thoughts on what we want instead of continually fixating on the reality of what we don't want?

Many authors explain this concept in comprehensive yet easy-to-understand terms. I have included a list of resources at the end of the book if you would like more information. Try to move past your logical and rational mind. Your mind is a tool, but it will limit you if it is not utilized correctly. The ego's role is to keep us under control, and it does not like when we venture into uncharted territory. However, it is here where life really begins.

By embracing these ideas, we find our perceptions of our experiences change—even if nothing else around us does. This new perception creates change in our future experiences. We learn that we are not dependent upon other people, events, or circumstances to define us. We find that our power lies within ourselves, and that is where we gain peace, joy, and fulfillment. The luxuries of money, status, power, or possessions do not define us. They, like our bodies, are only temporary.

We are meant to live abundant, healthy, joyous lives filled with creative endeavors designed to help us—and our universe— grow. When we find this place inside of ourselves, our outer reality changes to match that vibration. We can experience joy and peace if we choose. We can create prosperity and perfect health. We can have loving relationships and fulfilling careers. And we are deserving of all of those. We are worthy of all of life's blessings—that is what we need to teach our children.

Claiming the power to choose our thoughts, beliefs, feelings and the words we use in the present means we now have the ability to create the lives we want in the future.

Focus your attention on one of your goals. State your strong intention to achieve this goal, and focus all of your awareness on it. Write down your goal in the present tense, beginning with the words "I am." Use plenty of positive emotion in your statement. (I am so grateful that...) Think of the goal in a positive light, imagining how you would feel if this goal came to fruition. If doubts begin to surface, acknowledge them, release them, and refocus your thoughts. Read this statement as many times during the day as you can, particularly when you arise and before going to bed. Visualize your goal coming to fruition—do not worry about the details or how it will happen. Think about it, speak about it, and envision your goal in a positive light. Feel as much gratitude as you can while you are envisioning the event. Feel as if it has already happened!

An Open Mind

We must view young people not as empty bottles to be filled but as candles to be lit.

—Robert Shaffer, retired chairman of the Department
of College Student Personnel Administration

SIXTEEN-YEAR-OLD MALALA YOUSAFZAI of Pakistan began to receive death threats from the Taliban when she voiced her opinion about the difficulty of living under Muslim rule. Policies forbidding girls from going to school, listening to music, or taking most jobs had been imposed, and Malala was known for her activism and advocacy of education for girls. A gunman shot her in the head and neck on her school bus, and after recuperating; she was asked what she thought the response to this should be. Malala shared that striking back would mean there is no difference between them and us. "You must fight others through peace and through dialogue and through education."

Our children are given the gift of exposure to many learning experiences throughout their lives; however, our current education system frequently misses the mark by not using this platform to foster children's natural curiosity or to hone critical-thinking skills. We have implemented so many standards for our children to attain that students, even at a young age, complain of stress and anxiety related to these assessments. Although they have been implemented with the intention of increasing the level of achievement for our nation's students, I wonder what the long-term repercussions of these programs will be, particularly for students who struggle academically.

It is my hope that your children's learning experiences do not stop with geography, multiplication tables, and rules of grammar. It is not to discount the importance in their growth, but to suggest that an alternate area of growth is just as significant. Learning about ourselves, our universe, and how they interrelate is essential. We discover an invaluable aspect of learning when we look below the surface of an event to the deeper meaning that it holds.

Teach your children to be open to new experiences and new concepts since we cannot always predict the manner in which important lessons appear. When new information resonates with them, help them trust those feelings. If they are only taught to trust what others tell them is important, how will they make decisions that are right for them in the future? If we answer with "because I said so" or "do what I say," how will they learn to use critical-thinking skills when they have their own choices to make? Let them question the information given to them, even from you and from their teachers.

Just as I am writing about principles in parenting that I think are important, you have to decide what is right for you. When something is right for you, it will stick. We have to give our children permission to do the same, even though they are only children. They need the space to make choices that are right for them, even if they differ from ours. These choices could result in lower grade point averages, fewer accolades, or difficult situations, but the lessons they will provide will be priceless.

Our growth often comes from the more difficult things we go through. The first step is to acknowledge that there is often more beyond the outward appearance of an event than we often realize. When we look closer, we find deeper meaning and notice synchronicities. If you look back at different times in your life, you can see where you may have understood more about life as the result of difficult experiences, some of which may have required you to change your way of viewing the world if it did not serve you anymore.

We want our children to be open to these new experiences, to evolve and grow, to question and consider possibilities, and to honor their intellectual curiosity—not to remain stagnant and set in their ways. This outlook will help your children the most—to see life as the adventure it is and to learn from all of their experiences, both positive and negative.

In every experience, even the most difficult, we can come away with more insight than we had before—if we are brave enough to do some soul-searching. This is true education.

. . . .

Remember a time when your children wanted to make a decision that you did not agree with. How did that situation work out? The next time this occurs, try stepping back and let them own the decision. Examine the consequences afterwards. Would you make that decision again?

. . . .

21

The Difficult Child

To truly grow, you have to be willing at any moment to sacrifice what you are for what you can be.

—Charles Dubois, Swiss neuropathologist and author

YOUR DIFFICULT CHILD is the one you love beyond measure. This child is also the one you don't like sometimes, the one who challenges your perception of yourself and your world, and the one who won't fall in line. This is the child who you profess not to understand, the one who embarrasses you, or the one who defies you at every turn. This may be the one whose lifestyle choices worry you, who shuts you out, who cannot seem to ever sit still, or the one who demands too much of your attention.

Our children have agendas, and as our lives intersect, their issues become tangled with our issues. It feels like they are standing in the way of our happiness, but that is never the case. They may disappoint us, but only if we hold them to a standard they cannot embrace. *Our children are not capable of giving us what we need—only we can do that.*

This situation is there for a reason, and it has to do with the growth that will help you both evolve. This precious opportunity holds information that can turn your life around. It can help identify the areas of your life that need more balance. You may need to become more patient, more tolerant, or more supportive. You may need to let go more or hold on tighter. Whether you agree with their actions or not, this child is challenging you to look at life through another lens. Know that this experience can teach you so much—and that the relationship contains lessons you both need to learn.

Examine the reasons you feel frustrated or angry, and look at the buttons it pushes. Where does this child challenge how you think about yourself? In what areas might you need to let go of control and move to acceptance? Do they remind you of parts of yourself you would rather not face?

You have to move past your resistance to find a place of forgiveness and acceptance for the child who does not do as you want. All of our interactions with others, but particularly those of our family system, have lessons for us to learn if we are open to them. Our relationships are a direct reflection of how we interact with the world, and there is tremendous growth to be gained from the awareness we unearth here. Look at this relationship, and examine what you feel is lacking. Whatever we feel someone is not giving to us is the very thing we are not giving to them. This is not easy to accept, and we create many excuses not to face the truth behind that statement, but this realization is the key to changing the situation.

Remember that we can only change ourselves, not anyone else. Everything is energy, and everything is in a state of flux and flow, including our relationships. We often find that when we change the energy we exude, if we are observant, we notice that others change around us as a result. In a place of acceptance, comprised of unconditional love—free of judgment, conditions, guilt, and punishment—we create deep transformations in our troubled relationships. It is only in this place that true transformation can occur, for us and for another.

This difficult child has much to teach you, and you have much to give them if you are open to negotiating methods of parenting that may not be working this time. Rather than ignoring the situation or trying to maintain an inauthentic relationship with this child, look to yourself first.

Examine where the difficulty really comes from and why it hits home; this introspection may surprise and enlighten you.

· ·

Think of your difficult child and dig deep to find ways that he or she pushes you to evolve, grow, and change your perception of who you are. The next time your difficult child challenges you, stop and ask yourself if you can look at the situation through a more objective lens. How can you alter your typical reaction to this situation to help you define who you truly are? How can you meet the behavior with love for the child and for yourself?

· ·

Your Children Have
Chosen You

*It's not only children who grow. Parents do too. As much as
we watch to see what our children do with their lives, they are
watching us to see what we do with ours. I can't tell my children
to reach for the sun. All I can do is reach for it myself.*

—Joyce Maynard, American author

WE MAY ASSUME that we are born to a certain set of parents
by chance, but I believe we choose both our parents and our
children. We are brought together because these relationships will
precipitate our highest growth. It is hard for people to believe they
may have chosen to experience problematic family situations, but
it does provide the basis for thought. Look at your children, and
try to imagine why you have been brought together. Look at your
parents, and do the same.

Consider children who have come into this world to learn
to stand up for their beliefs and choices, to honor their truths. A
gay child who decides to defend his or her sexual orientation will
learn this lesson well. The child's parent may have chosen to learn
a lesson of tolerance and understanding. We are all here to help
each other evolve. If we choose not to learn from the lessons these
relationships teach us, we can be assured we will be presented
with more difficult avenues to learn them.

Our relationships with our children and our parents provide
perfect opportunities for us to heal the places within ourselves
that need it the most. Our higher selves have orchestrated an

assignment with other people who play significant roles in our lives. We have come together to help each other reach heights in our growth that we could not reach alone. As it states in *A Course in Miracles*, these relationships are our syllabus. These partnerships do not occur randomly; they are carefully orchestrated for a higher purpose, the evolution of both parties.

A young lady from El Salvador entered high school in eleventh grade, speaking little English. Carla lived with her father, but he worked long hours and did not have much time to give her. She began her classes with the intent of being an excellent student. She studied hard and took advantage of all the opportunities provided to her. Any challenges Carla faced were met with determination and diligence. She graduated with honors and entered a community college, taking the bus there every day and working after school to pay for her expenses. This young lady, who entered the country with little education and a poor command of the English language, transferred to Columbia University and graduated three years later. The obstacles she was presented with fostered her drive, perseverance, and fierce commitment. If Carla were provided with all she needed from the start, these character traits would have no need to grow. Perhaps her father's lesson was to be inspired by his daughter's tenacity and ability to create a life of her choosing. The agreements we make with our parents before we arrive on this planet offer both parties the perfect platform to experience what we need to evolve.

Writing those words prompted me to consider my own path. Why would I choose my own set of parents in this lifetime? After I found myself experiencing some anger over that thought, it dawned on me. Why would I choose a father who was emotionally distant, derisive, and physically absent most of my life? A father who made me uncomfortable with sexual innuendo and inappropriate comments? When I look at the father my husband is to our children, I realize how blessed they are. While I am grateful for that, I also experience a feeling of loss because it shows me what I missed. Why would I choose a mother who, while loving and kind, was more concerned about how things looked than how they were, operating mainly in a state of denial?

I looked closer and found a few very good reasons. My upbringing has helped me understand and support students who are dealing with difficult family situations in my role as school counselor. It has been part of what prompted me to write a book on a topic that I feel passionate about and that I hope will be of service to parents and children. It has helped me forgive my parents for the imperfections of their parenting as I forgave myself for the imperfections of my own. I have learned to increase my own self-love and compassion for others—and to reach a deeper level of understanding about the world and myself.

When I look at the whole picture—not just the pieces—I see that my father had his demons, coming from a chaotic home riddled with alcoholism and abuse. I can picture him, confused and afraid as a child, growing up without the nurturing and support necessary to become an emotionally healthy adult. I understand how he may have kept his distance to protect me from feelings he didn't want to act upon. I also understand that he did his best, as we all do, and I choose to forgive him as well as my mother. I appreciate the moments that were noble, the love that was there when I looked, and the fact that my father often worked two jobs to support our family. I can see how it fits together, what I have learned, and how I have evolved.

The reasons why we choose our parents and children are complex, but both parties evolve and grow because of this union—if they choose to do the work this growth entails. The forgiveness and acceptance we grant to others always affects us in positive ways. We are all connected, and every time we make a choice based in love, the universe rejoices.

I truly understand the importance of good parenting, the significance of our roles and how, as a society, we need to consider some new parenting strategies while we keep the ones that benefit our children. Along the way, we need to know we are all doing our best, and to practice acceptance and understanding for others and ourselves on a daily basis.

Even the experiences you would not call optimal have caused your children's growth in some way. As your children navigate your family system, they develop skills and strengths that will help them deal with life in the larger community. Families provide all types of experiences—both positive and negative. Look at your children, and see how they have grown from the experiences within your family.

Think about how perfect it is that you are together and how you continue to learn from each other every day.

. . . .

Get a pen and paper. Take a few moments to consider these questions and write down the first answers that come to you: What have you learned from being born into your own family? How has it shaped your life? What strengths, skills, or insights did you develop?

How have your children benefitted from being your children? In what areas have they grown or learned lessons? What have you learned from them?

. . . .

Authenticity

To be nobody but yourself in a world which is doing its best, night and day, to make you everybody else means to fight the hardest battle any human being can fight; and never stop fighting.

—E. E. Cummings, American poet,
painter, essayist, and playwright

BEING AUTHENTIC ENTAILS being honest and secure enough to be who you truly are, and it requires that you consistently make choices that bring you joy. It takes time to find this place because we have been programmed to please others: our parents (no matter how old we are), teachers, religious leaders, doctors, and friends. We get the message that their happiness depends upon our actions. Why do we let others' perceptions define what we know is right for us? Time and again, we sell out our own self-worth in exchange for the approval of others. Authenticity is knowing who we are and claiming it. Teaching our children the value of being genuine, despite the ever-changing whims of those around them, is priceless.

The topic of authenticity brings to mind a student named Miguel. He came to the high school in eleventh grade from a school district that had problems including poverty, violence, drugs, and gang activity. His mother, a single parent, relocated Miguel and his younger brothers to the school district because she was concerned about the violence that was prevalent in their neighborhood. She saw some signs that worried her; Miguel was doing poorly in school, was truant on many occasions, and was getting into fights.

What his mother did not realize was that he was already being recruited for a gang he was seriously considering joining.

Miguel's mother worked two jobs to support her family, and he was responsible for watching his brothers and helping out around the house. Miguel was angry with his father for abandoning the family and not supporting them. He was angry with his mother for uprooting him and for all the responsibilities he had to assume. It was a rude awakening for Miguel, entering a high school where the teachers cared if he was in class and if he was learning, a place where he was given the space to decide what he wanted.

Discussions with Miguel did not reflect a young man without morals, one who was prone to violence, or one who had no goals. Our discussions revealed an angry young man that was deeply hurt by his father's abandonment and overwhelmed by his responsibilities. Miguel did not see many options available to him, but he was limited more by his perception of his experience than his actual circumstances. We worked together to explore what he wanted out of life, and we investigated possibilities that he did not know existed. Because Miguel was open to change, he was able to discover his authentic self, the one that was hidden under layers of defenses, but this did not happen until he chose to let go of the way others defined him to make room for who he truly was. When we discovered that he had aspirations of becoming a pilot, we researched available programs. His grades improved, and he was accepted into an aviation program at a local college where he began to pursue his dreams.

Miguel's authentic self was able to appear when he was open to exploring who he was—without needing validation from others. He moved beyond his anger and feelings of inadequacy to find his self-worth. Now evident, it had the space to emerge and guide him to who he truly was.

We need to accept our children as they are, to give them the space to question what is right for them and the room to explore what they really feel and want. Once they embrace self-acceptance, it is priceless. This place will guide us to what we want, what we truly desire, and what is right for us. As Farrah Gray, American businessman and motivational speaker so aptly put it, "Build your own dreams or someone else will hire you to build theirs." Funny, but not when we apply it to our own lives.

When we acknowledge our truth, we can demonstrate the security it brings us for our children. You are the role model for your children, and they benefit when you show them through your words and actions that you are secure in who you are. We enjoy enormous freedom when we let go of the need for approval from others, even those we love and respect. If they live their lives authentically, our children will not grow up with the excessive need to please, which is a chronic problem in today's society, particularly for girls.

Authenticity is where we find our gifts, where we allow ourselves to be the person we were meant to be.

• •

In what areas do you want to improve your own level of authenticity? Consider some ways you can do this. The next time you have the opportunity, make a choice that reflects this and examine your reaction afterwards.

• •

Feelings

The best way out is always through.

—Robert Frost, American poet

MY FRIEND WORKED with a man who was perpetually angry. Her colleague would often storm through their office, overreacting to all kinds of situations. This man was never pleasant; anger and bitterness emanated from him at all times, and people tended to avoid him because he was in a constant state of irascibility. While arriving at work one day, my friend discovered that her colleague had a massive heart attack the night before. Although physically healthy, his system could not take the overload of negativity and anger. This was a wake-up call for him; he was given the opportunity to evaluate how he was dealing with his problems and how he was living his life.

Feelings can be messy. They take time and patience, but your children have them—and you do as well. Unacknowledged and repressed, feelings can grow and fester until they wreak havoc in our lives. It is important to let your children own their feelings and not give them the impression that they are wrong. If that happens, they will repress them, which lead to guilt, frustration, anger, and acting out.

An example of a healthy expression of feelings is when your son shares his vulnerability and wants to cry. It is illustrated when your daughter is angry and doesn't want to change to please others, including you. Disconnection to their feelings can lead to children who are unable to identify how they feel as well as being at a loss to know how to handle situations when they are angry or hurt. They may grow into adults who use food, shopping, or television to cover up feelings they do not know how to deal with. They may self-medicate with drugs or alcohol. They may turn into men who feel it is not acceptable to acknowledge their vulnerability or women who don't take time to acknowledge what they really want because they are too busy meeting everyone else's needs

Your children have a right to their feelings, and so do you. Acknowledge and validate when you are disappointed, overwhelmed, or afraid. Let your children see that these feelings are acceptable and not necessary to conceal.

When we give ourselves permission to allow and experience our feelings, they lose their power over us. We believe these feelings are us, but they are not. They are transient expressions that do not define who we truly are. Our feelings are visitors who have come to tell us something important. They will leave after we listen to what they say, unless we hold them hostage.

We have choices about what to feel and what to do with our feelings; they do not own us. They are to be acknowledged and respected, not incorporated into who we think we are. Just like every situation in life, we have choices about how to approach this one as well. We get misled because our feelings are so deep and internal. It seems as though we are them, but we are something much grander, much more permanent. If we do not realize this, and we let them take over, they will affect what we do in all areas of our lives.

You can look at the messages your feelings bring, work on changing what you can, and then decide to accept the rest. True growth stems from the acceptance and resolution of painful feelings, and sometimes you just have to delve into them and deal with them. You can do so, knowing that they will not dissolve otherwise and that you will not fall apart as you confront them. But if you avoid your feelings, they will always find a way to surface—in a healthy way or otherwise. Unacknowledged, they can lead to rifts in relationships, unwise decision-making, or health crises. When you move through them, as uncomfortable as this may be, you always leave the process stronger and healthier.

You can be a role model for your children by demonstrating that you have a right to the feelings that life's challenges bring. They will watch whether or not you pay attention to the messages your feelings bring about how you are living your life. Show your children how to accept and release their emotions so they are able to dissipate. You can help them by displaying healthy ways of resolving your feelings, such as talking about them, crying, journaling, meditating, or expressing them though exercise, dance, art or music.

The most important aspect is to recognize that we all have feelings; they are not wrong, and they do not define who we are.

. . . .

Examine your feelings right now. Are they comfortable or uncomfortable? Accept these feelings, recognizing that they are here to give you information about your life. Be cognizant of these feelings, but do not own them. Let them pass through you, learning from them while letting them dissipate. The next time you experience an uncomfortable feeling, be an observer. Try to look at the situation objectively, looking at the cause and your reaction. Then choose to let the feeling go. What can you learn from this approach? Is the experience less painful this way?

. . . .

The Perfect Parent

Our strength grows out of our weaknesses.

—Ralph Waldo Emerson, American
essayist, lecturer, and poet

WHAT DOES THE perfect parent look like? One who has unlimited patience or who always sacrifices their own desires for their child's? One who can provide luxuries or the highest quality education? One who is present in all interactions and always accepts their children as they are?

Of course we know that there is no such creature, but so often we judge ourselves for not being perfect. We compare ourselves with others whose families appear ideal or with whatever image we conjure up when we think of the model parent. Quite honestly, we all have our shares of regrets and disappointments with our own parents, our children, and ourselves.

I have seen good, caring people who remain stuck in a place of regret over what they consider to be their limitations as parents. They fixate in this place of disappointment over their imperfections and the effect they have on their children. By staying in that place, they miss out on all the wonderful occurrences that are taking place right now. I have been down that road myself, and when I revisit there, I am reminded that it is not an enjoyable place.

There is no perfect parent or perfect child, and we are much harder on ourselves than we would ever be on anyone else. We aim our focus at our so-called faults and easily dismiss the magnificent moments. We have to learn to forgive ourselves for what we consider to be our shortcomings in order to forgive our children for not being who we want them to be. This connection is highly significant, and its symbiotic relationship is non-negotiable.

Parenting is a tough job and a daunting enterprise. Although we know there is a lot at stake, we forge ahead anyway with hope in our hearts that the rewards will be wonderful. They are, but we have to be ready to ride the waves that take us to that place. Perhaps our own childhood experiences were not ideal or we lacked great role models; we might have that to sort through. We may find it difficult to balance the needs of others with of the responsibilities life entails. It is a position that demands great sacrifice, both physical and emotional, as well as great patience. It is important for us to give ourselves a break and not dwell on regrets.

Sometimes our parenting is glorious, and other times it is not, but guilt over our imperfections keeps us caged in a prison that holds our self-love hostage. Guilt tells us that the basis of who we are is inherently immoral and flawed—that we are not deserving of compassion, forgiveness, and love. Nothing could be farther from the truth, and people's beliefs in their own unworthiness cause the majority of problems in their lives.

Learn from your mistakes, and move on to being the parent you want to be in the present; that is the greatest gift you can give your child. Show your children that they are always lovable and worthy and that mistakes are a part of learning. Demonstrate this by forgiving them and yourself for mistakes and misdeeds. Help your children embrace the self-love that is their inherent birthright by acknowledging that perfection is an elusive goal. Show them that they are perfect just as they are.

Our imperfections and mistakes make us real; they are the stepping-stones that help us discover our truth and lead to our growth.

In what area do you need to forgive your child? Yourself? What do these imperfections teach you? Is forgiveness something you want? Think of several ways that holding onto unforgiveness is affecting your life.

Raising Children
With Character

Too often we underestimate the power of a touch, a smile, a kind word, a listening ear, an honest compliment, or the smallest act of caring, all of which have the potential to turn a life around.

> —Leo F. Buscaglia, American author, motivational
> speaker, and professor of special education

IN JANUARY 2013, Spanish athlete Ivan Fernandez Anaya was running a race against Kenyan runner, Abel Mutai, in Madrid, Spain. Mutai was leading the race but stopped before the finish line, not realizing he didn't cross the line. Not understanding Spanish, he didn't grasp that the spectators were encouraging him to continue. Trailing Mutai in the race, Fernandez Anaya ran up to him and showed him where to cross so he could win the race. In an interview after the race, Fernandez Anaya said his heart told him it was the right thing to do.

Kindness is underrated. Our society has taught us that it is important to be aggressive in the pursuit of our goals. We are told not to let anything stand in our way, not to take no for an answer, and that the end justifies the means. Commitment is fine, and pursuing a goal has merit, but it is never necessary to trample on other people to attain our goals. The kind child, the one who is sensitive or quiet, or the one who doesn't want to hurt others is sometimes ostracized or ridiculed.

Why is kindness seen as a form of weakness in our society?

Why do we feel that we have to drive aggressively and pass others on the road? Why is it necessary to be the smartest one in the class or acceptable to demean others in the workplace to get ahead? It doesn't have to be this way. We can teach our children that they can achieve their goals while being kind to others and forming supportive relationships. We can demonstrate that working together leads to greater gains for all of us. We can model values such as kindness, empathy, and respect, and we can demonstrate those values by how we treat others in the scope of our days. Let your children know that the messages they give out are what they get back. Our good deeds restore balance to the world; they contribute to the positive flow of energy from one soul to another, and demonstrating compassion is how one soul honors another.

As we encounter others throughout our day, we don't know the depth of their difficulties. The person waiting in front of us at the supermarket checkout line might be heartbroken after losing a spouse to cancer, devastated after the loss of his or her home to foreclosure, or feeling the disorientation of returning home after military service. The waitress serving us tonight may have been up all night with a child who is ill or may have just found out she lost her job. The mail carrier you greet every day might have been told he has a terminal disease. The act of kindness you give to someone you cross paths with may seem small to you, but it just might be the seed that allows faith to grow in someone's heart again. Our gesture of compassion is sorely needed, and the effect we have on each other is profound.

Teaching our children about character is an important part of their educations. The importance of respect for others, fairness, compassion, integrity, and honesty gets overlooked on too many occasions in the education of our children, but your children learn most by what they are taught at home. Show your children that how we treat others is ultimately a measure of how much respect we have for ourselves—true respect, not ego-based conceit.

Emphasize how important it is to do the right thing, to be kind to others, and to stand up for someone else when they need you, even when no one is looking. The purpose of doing so is not to get something in return, but because it is the right thing to do. Everything we do is imbued with the intention behind our actions, and it has a direct effect on the outcome of any of our choices. Let's teach our children about the importance of aligning our values with our actions, infusing them with altruism and authenticity. This type of education will lead to children who grow to be empowered, capable, and secure adults.

These are the people who will make great contributions to the many areas of our society that are in desperate need of true leadership.

· ·

Pick a time when you choose to consciously practice compassion throughout every encounter in your day. Evaluate the effect this had on you and those you interacted with.

Where have you seen your children demonstrate character? How did that situation turn out for them?

· ·

Patience

Have patience with all things, but first of all, with yourself.

—Saint Francis de Sales, Roman Catholic saint

ONE OF MY regrets as a parent is feeling that I was not patient enough at times and that I overreacted at the small stuff—things that children do because they are children, things that wouldn't matter in ten minutes or ten years. This did not occur often, but when it happened, it made me feel out of control and that I should act better toward those I loved the most.

There are days as a parent when it feels as if every force in the universe is competing for your time and energy. There are times when everyone wants a piece of you, and your children always want the biggest piece, as they should. You feel overwhelmed as you are pulled in a million directions. You wish someone else could make a decision, get everything done, and pick up the pieces. You think that if you hear one more whine, one more complaint, or witness one more fight between siblings, you will blow. And sometimes you do, and it is not a pretty sight when you let loose all the stuff you have bottled up on your unsuspecting children.

I've done it. We all have. It happens because we are imperfect human beings with faults and limits. We make mistakes, but we do the best we can with the skill and knowledge we have at the time. We have to be more cognizant of those times when we are starting to feel overwhelmed, and it is important to look for some cues; we may become withdrawn, curt, or anxious. We may have to ask for help, take a walk, or take a bath. Perhaps the first step is to make peace with the knowledge that we are doing the best we can.

Know that our children do more than survive our shortcomings. They actually become stronger and more resilient, more able to handle the people they meet in their day that are angry, irritating, or overreacting. They become able to deal with the imperfections in their worlds without falling apart because they have seen them in us—and they know that unconditional love lies underneath those faults. They know we are imperfect and that we have given them permission to be as well because they have seen that perfection is an elusive virtue. Our children realize that love survives in the wake of a storm.

Is patience a virtue? It certainly is, and nowhere is it more tested than in the role of parent. We need to be patient with our children, but we also need to remember not to let everything pile up, not to disregard the ticking time bomb. It is not pleasant for our children to experience our outbursts, but they will rebound and learn from the experience.

Our own misgivings over those impatient moments are harder on us than our children, and as we review our roles as parent, we have to forgive ourselves for them.

. . . .

This week, if you find yourself feeling aggravated or impatient, find a place where you can be alone for a minute. Take five long breaths—in through your nose and out through your mouth. With each breath, think of something you are grateful for in your life. Feel deep gratitude for these circumstances, and remind yourself that this moment of impatience will pass.

. . . .

Expectations

When I was five years old, my mother always told me that happiness was the key to life. When I went to school, they asked me what I wanted to be when I grew up. I wrote down "happy." They told me I didn't understand the assignment, and I told them they didn't understand life.

—John Lennon, English musician, singer, and songwriter

I HAVE WORKED in school districts where parental expectations were high; the majority of students excelled in classes, and a grade of C was not cause for celebration. That being said, there were a lot of resources offered to students, and they knew their parents and teachers supported them in the goal of a higher education.

There have been some instances where I felt the level of expectation was difficult for the students. Sara was taking a challenging high school curriculum that required her to work extremely hard. Each year, we would meet with her parents to go over the schedule of classes to ensure that it was filled with rigor. I could see that her existence was filled with many pressures, and Sara would consistently look to her parents to answer any question that was asked of her.

This young lady had a skin condition that was exacerbated by anxiety, and it appeared to me that the majority of her day was stressful. I did not see any room for the real person behind this façade to emerge. Sara's activity resume was replete with accomplishments that were carefully orchestrated to create the persona of a young woman filled with drive and determination. Discussion with her did not reflect these characteristics at all. I often wondered what Sara really felt and actually wanted. I don't know that this question was ever honestly answered.

Dan underwent open-heart surgery to correct a genetic defect while in ninth grade and had a difficult recovery due to medical complications. He returned to high school the next year and proceeded to do well in his classes. Dan came to see me because he was experiencing test anxiety in his science class. It turned out that Dan's parents were placing a great deal of pressure on him to do well in chemistry, and the C he was getting for the quarter did not measure up. There were discussions about taking away privileges, such as the computer, phone, and time with friends.

These parents were not unlikable or uncaring individuals. They cared very much for their child's well-being. What makes well-intentioned, loving parents react in this manner? It may relate to fear that their children will not be successful or that there are limits on what is available for their child. They may feel that their own self-worth is determined by their children's accomplishments. At times, they are fearful that they cannot control their children's actions or do not have enough faith in their children's decisions.

We all know people who live their lives on automatic pilot, going from responsibility to obligation, never really present in their lives and never gaining insight from their experiences. Don't we want more for our children?

These beliefs are solidly entrenched in not recognizing that our children are enough just as they are and that they are able to direct their lives—much more than we give them credit for. There is a lack of understanding that this is their training ground and that we have to let them find out what makes them happy. If we orchestrate every move they make, how will they ever learn what is right for them?

Let go, have faith, and surrender to the process of accepting your children as they are.

What do your children really want? Take the time to ask them, and most importantly, take the time to listen to their answers. Don't let your fear or worry get in the way of their dreams.

Teenagers

Adolescence is perhaps nature's way of preparing parents to welcome the empty nest.

—Karen Savage and Patricia Adams, authors

TEENAGERS CAN BE beastly; they can be sarcastic and rude, self-centered and opinionated, bossy and egotistical. They are not doing this intentionally; they are fighting to discover their identities. It is their unique process for figuring out who they are and how they fit into our world. They have to be this way to protect their emerging independence, which is being threatened by the power we have over their lives.

It's funny how, all of a sudden, we are not as smart or interesting as we used to be. It's not personal, and taking offense will make this transition more difficult for all involved. A sense of humor is highly recommended as you travel through this phase; it is important to keep things in perspective and not overreact.

Your teenager still needs you to set reasonable limits, and you do them no favor by greeting rude behavior with open arms. But understand that it is an uneasy time for your child, knowing they are on their way to adulthood and that soon they will be the captains of their own ships. They have to make it look like you don't know what you are doing so their decisions will stand a chance. They seem as if they don't care about what you think so they can figure out what they really think. They have to start to detach so they can stand on their own when the time comes. If they don't practice this now, their independence day will come anyway—and they will not be ready.

This is when you have to practice the delicate art of holding on and letting go at the same time, of giving your children room to explore while keeping them connected. You might feel like asserting your authority even more at this point, but no one wins when it turns into a power struggle. I have danced this dance with my own children, and I see it reenacted every year as the new group of ninth graders enters the high school, and the parents have difficulty adjusting to this new level of independence. It is like that new dance step you are trying to master; you take a few steps forward and a few back, make a misstep, and find your balance again. It is a learning process for both parties.

Your children still need you, and you can't cling too tightly, but don't let them push you away either. Make it a point to spend time with them even when they tell you that you embarrass them. Don't take it personally, and remember that they still love you; you are allowed to take pleasure in knowing that they will embarrass their own children one day. I remember when my daughter told my husband and me that she was grateful we didn't "completely" embarrass her in front of her friends.

You have to keep your children's confidences when they share information with you and not overreact, because if you do, you will not be the one they turn to next time. They will go through phases and style changes, and this is an area where less reaction is sometimes better. Let them work it out for themselves, or they may dig their heels in deeper. For example, although they deny it, I found that my daughters' tattoos multiplied exponentially in response to my objections to them.

When you taught your children to ride a bicycle, after many practice runs, there was a time when you had to let go, cross your fingers, and hope for the best. It's kind of like that now. It is hard for parents to let go of the control their children so valiantly fight for, but at some point, *we have to trust in the values we have instilled in our children.* This does not mean we will stop worrying or that we have no say in what goes on. It just means we have to be brave enough to give them room to grow. It is the natural progression of their development, and although we tend to focus on the problems they may encounter, we ultimately want our children to be strong and self-sufficient. We don't want them to be afraid to live their lives without us, and our children need the courage they get from our blessings to make this transition.

Although your relationship with your children changes, and there is a sense of loss that you feel because of this, your bond can grow into something stronger and more extraordinary. You will find a sense of quiet satisfaction as you watch your children deal with the situations that life entails—at times still looking for your reassurance and support—but only when you are not looking. They need you always; the reasons and intensity may change, and your relationship may take some twists and turns, but you have much to teach your teenage children and much to learn from them. Communicate, make it a point to spend time together, forgive each other, be honest, and be open to listening to each other.

Change and growth are part of every facet of our lives, and it is nowhere more evident than in the parent-child relationship. Change is inevitable—to resist it is a wasteful use of time and emotion.

Embrace it instead, and meet up on the other side of this transition as adults who have a solid level of respect and love for each other.

· ·

As your children grow, try to embrace the changes that this transition brings.

Recall your own teenage years and the angst you felt. While times have changed, many aspects of growing up have not. Try to recall how you felt growing up; your children's experiences are not much different.

· ·

Sex, Drugs, And
Rock 'N' Roll

*Self-esteem is made up of primarily of two things: feeling lovable
and feeling capable.*

—Jack Canfield, American motivational
speaker and author

I REMEMBER INITIATING a discussion with my younger daughter
about sex. She was about ten years old, and I thought I was being
proactive. I remember giving her a lot of information, but every
piece of information was answered with, "I know that already."
I realized I had waited too long.

Your children need information about topics such as this at an
early age. You will be able to assess how much to discuss by the
questions your children ask, but remember to answer honestly and
never leave a question unanswered. It is much better for them to
receive accurate information from you. It is also a good idea to
take advantage of everyday opportunities that happen naturally
and use them to connect with subjects you want to bring up.

The reality is that children are experimenting with drugs,
using alcohol, and becoming sexually active at earlier ages than
ever. This may have to do with a feeling of disconnection from
family, school, or community; it may stem from a lack of self-
esteem, which leads them to seek approval in another way. Many
teenagers are experiencing a desire to numb feelings that have been
repressed and are now painful to acknowledge. They are having
difficulty navigating our world with the expectations placed upon

children at younger ages. Others decide to experiment with the belief that they are invincible.

The reasons are varied and numerous. What I know for sure is that your children will be given the opportunity to get involved with at-risk behavior at an early age and that you are their best insulation against this. They are seeking connection, a feeling of belonging, validation for their feelings, and most importantly, self-acceptance. They need reasonable limits, consistency, and stability, but they also need a place where they feel they belong. Fear in regard to the consequences of unsafe behavior will not be enough for them to make good choices. They need to feel disinterested in participating in the first place, and this comes from a place of security and not seeking happiness or love from artificial sources.

Your children will watch how you handle stress in your own life. They will notice if you wash away the difficulties of your day with a few beers at night or if you use shopping as a way to get an immediate adrenaline rush. They will watch as you satisfy your need for love with chocolate or if you don't sit still long enough to assess how you are feeling. They will look on as you work eighty hours a week to avoid dealing with your life. Change begins with honesty and awareness. We are our children's role models, and it is important to look at ourselves truthfully.

I remember when a student told me she was seven months pregnant. She was fourteen years old at the time and waited to tell anyone because she wanted to have the child. This young girl was an only child living with an elderly mother in abject poverty; her life was very lonely. She was looking for someone to love, and she wanted someone who would love her back. Having a child was the only way she saw to accomplish this.

The best deterrents for behavior that places your children at risk are the love and connection that develop within your family and a strong sense of security and self-confidence within your child. Your children will seek out this feeling of self-acceptance and connection; if they cannot find it within your family, they will seek out other situations that satisfy this need.

Allow for an expression of feelings, and provide healthy choices. Allow your home to be a safe haven where you can model values that are important for your child.

· ·

Begin an open discussion with your children about the issues discussed above. Be open to answering questions honestly, having a non-judgmental discussion, and creating a tolerant, respectful space for future concerns or questions.

· ·

Creativity

We all have two choices. We can make a living or we can design a life.

—Jim Rohn, American entrepreneur,
author, and motivational speaker

CREATION IS OUR strongest drive—the need to express ourselves fully. We create ourselves over again in every moment, defining what we stand for by our choices and our actions. We are never stagnant, never in the same place as the moment before. Our entire existence is based on a state of change and growth; this desire is the essence of living, of being alive. The impulse to create again, even after our creations have come to fruition, is the driving force of our lives. As physician and author Deepak Chopra said, "The most creative act you will ever undertake is the act of creating yourself."

The ways to express our creativity are diverse; one might be a talented artist, another a wonderful cook, and someone else may be an inspiring motivational speaker. The artist inspires a multitude of feelings in us as we experience the messages portrayed in their work. The chef produces mouth-watering dishes that fill diners with contentment and comfort. Motivational speakers effect change in others as they help listeners get in touch with an awareness that needs to surface. Another individual creates a loving home, a garden where others find solace, or an inspirational company that cares for its employees.

Creation is as individual as we are. It is the God-given talent within us that is our gift to the world, another avenue for us to express love. Part of the soul's mission is to express and share these gifts while inspiring others to do the same, making our planet a better place. When I think of my mom and my younger daughter, I can see how being an artist is intrinsic to their being; it is a part of them that cannot be denied. My mother's artwork is exquisite, and she dedicated her life to this craft. She taught china painting in our basement for years, spending hours every day painting and creating. My younger daughter, Samantha, is the same way; artistic expression is in her bones. It is part of her genetic makeup, and not to nurture this would be to deny the gift that helps her express who she is. My older daughter, Jessica, is a talented pianist, and music in all forms has always been an integral part of her life.

Your children have gifts they are longing to express that are individual to them. Observing what makes them the happiest can lead to the discovery of these gifts. What makes your children lose all sense of time? What makes their hearts sing, and where do they find their joy? This longing and desire yearns to be expressed and released, and it is one of the most important reasons we are here on this planet at this time and place. If this desire to create is not expressed naturally, it will find a less beneficial way to express itself. Sadly, our lack of confidence and our emphasis on being responsible or practical often results in the denial of these gifts.

I recall a discussion with a colleague whose son was passionate about the field of environmental science. His son was majoring in this field in college, working in related internships, and volunteering in his free time, but he could not find a paid position. He shared that his son's eyes lit up when he spoke of his passion for this area; his son could talk for hours about protecting the environment, and it was all he wanted to do. My colleague was concerned that his son wouldn't be able to get a job and worried about his desire to continue this field in graduate school. He was being advised to guide his son to find a different path with more employment potential, but he felt conflicted about this advice.

It is disappointing that we have so little faith in our children and ourselves. Why would we ever want to discourage this type of passion? Instead of encouraging our children to be realistic, logical, and practical, help them believe they can attain their dreams, express their creative desires, and live a life of their choosing. Do not neglect the talent your children have. It is a gift that their spirits as well as our world desperately needs.

Honor your children's creativity because this natural talent is their gift to the universe.

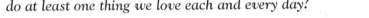

Embrace your children's creative nature, and encourage them to engage in an activity this week that they truly love. Do something that you love to do as well. Set aside a special time to explore this experience. Examine how you feel and consider whether this feeling carried over to your daily responsibilities.

How special could each day be if we made a commitment to do at least one thing we love each and every day?

A Love That Is Real

You may give them your love but not your thoughts, for they have their own thoughts.

—Khalil Gibran, Lebanese artist, poet, and writer

IT IS IMPOSSIBLE to love your children too much, but feelings that masquerade as love such as worry, authority, and control are not love; they are fear-based emotions that do not benefit your relationship with your children. Love is forgiveness, respect, and empathy. Real love is based in security, knowing who you truly are, and accepting others as they are.

Real love says, "You don't have to be like me or do what I want you to do. Be who you are, and be happy. Follow your bliss. Be yourself, and I will accept you as you are now and as you grow and change. I will support you in your choices, and I will be there to give you a hand you when you fall. You are not responsible for my happiness, but I will share my feelings with love when you cross boundaries and show you why it doesn't serve others or you. I will not let you treat others or me with disrespect because that does not serve either of us, but I will demonstrate this in a way that leaves us both feeling respected. I will accept you when you are angry or hurt and will not take these feelings personally. My love comes from a secure place that will not cling or control, and I will honor your development as you grow. I look upon this transition with understanding and acceptance, knowing that all things change and that love is the only thing remaining in their wake."

If we could bring ourselves to this place in parenting, our children would grow to be confident, empowered beings following their own paths of happiness while contributing their gifts to the world. They would openly claim their power of choice and would experience the freedom of living their lives as they choose. They would understand that utilizing our free will is truly the most important gift we can give to this universe. Our relationship with our children would grow and flourish based on mutual respect and integrity, not neediness or control. As teacher and author Neale Donald Walsch said, "When you love another for who they are, whether they give you what you need or not, then you truly love them."

Examples of real love surround us every day. Real love can be seen when a mother visits her homeless, mentally ill daughter on the street corner when she will not accept an offer of help. It is apparent as a father encourages his blind child to pursue her goal of living on the college campus, despite his own fears. It becomes clear when a couple makes a great sacrifice by relocating to another state to raise their sixteen-year-old nephew, left orphaned by a tragic accident. Real love is interested in what it can give, not what it can get.

We can show our children that we love them even when we don't like their behaviors. We can lend support in difficult times without directing their lives. We can demonstrate that our children are important and they matter, while also taking care of ourselves. We can help them understand that their happiness and self-worth are not dependent upon the actions or words of others, even ours.

The repercussions of this type of parenting would lead to healthier, more secure children who become healthier, more secure parents from which their own children would benefit, and so on.

. . . .

Recall a time when you practiced a love that was "real." How did that work out? What were the repercussions for you and your child? How did it affect your relationship?

. . . .

Health

Our bodies are our gardens—our wills are our gardeners.
—William Shakespeare, English poet and playwright

I CRINGE WHEN I think of the foods regularly given to my children as they were growing up: processed foods, sugar-laden products, and the not-so-occasional drive-through for a Happy Meal. I erroneously considered us healthy eaters because I cooked a homemade meal almost every night. I wish I knew more about nutrition years ago, although I am sure my children do not— they would have missed out on Marshmallow Alpha-bits and Gummy Worms. They consider me somewhat obsessed with natural products now, and I can't disagree. I wish I had taught my children healthy habits early on and modeled that for them in order to establish a healthy foundation.

I encourage you to take the time to learn sound nutritional practices. Take a class, read some books, look at websites, or work with a nutritionist. I have included valuable resources at the end of this book to assist you. It is important to know that sound nutrition can be attained on any budget and that making small changes is the first step. Learn about the importance of fruits and vegetables, organic foods, alkalinity in the body, and topics such as gluten sensitivity, food allergies, and genetically modified foods. Discover the importance of vitamins, minerals, supplements, functional medicine, exercise, the mind/body connection, yoga, and meditation. Help your children learn to respect their bodies and not abuse them with nicotine, drugs, excessive alcohol, or toxic foods. Recognize that our bodies are marvelous mechanisms, working hard for us every minute of every day. We take it for granted at times, but we have to acknowledge our responsibility to support and respect our body's process.

It is essential that we focus our energy and intention on appreciating this intricate system and assisting the body in reaching its natural state of wellness. A health crisis is often a wake-up call that conveys how we need to appreciate our bodies and respect what they need for optimal health. When our bodies are healthy, we have the energy and vitality to live our lives with purpose and joy. When we are feeling lethargic or ill, our attention is on those conditions, and we may lose focus on our self-growth or contributions to the world.

In 2005, *The New York Times* reported that for the first time, the current generation of children in America could have shorter life expectancies than their parents. Young children have a higher rate of obesity and chronic illness than ever before. Children are regularly being diagnosed with Type 2 diabetes, heart disease, high blood pressure, and high cholesterol—diseases once belonging primarily to adults. They have more allergies, higher incidences of asthma, migraines, and problematic skin conditions. I have seen more students than ever being diagnosed with cancer, and it needs to be acknowledged that cancer is of epidemic proportion within all facets of our population. It is not supposed to be this way; we have to recognize the connection between what we put in our bodies, our lifestyles, and our stress levels with the increase in disease of our nation's children and the rest of our society.

We also need to be cognizant of the connection between our minds and bodies—the fact that our thoughts, feelings, beliefs, and emotions play a starring role in the state of our physical health. We can make all the right health and lifestyle choices, but if we are in a constant state of unforgiveness, anger, lovelessness, or negativity, we will ultimately see this reflected in our bodies; all of our systems are intimately connected.

Children's eating habits and lifestyle choices are formed in a variety of ways, but they are primarily learned at home. The media plays a large part by marketing and advertising unhealthy options at every turn. Even school lunches could use an improvement. There are many areas that need improving, but the one you have control over is in your kitchen, your home, and what you model. Become knowledgeable about the many benefits of a healthy lifestyle and available nutritional choices.

Model healthy habits for your children, and they will take their main cues from you.

• •

Decide to make one healthy lifestyle change right now. Discuss this change with your family. Transformation can begin with one small step. Examine how this impacts you and your family. Is this a change you will decide to keep?

• •

The Greatest Gift

You are the closest I will ever come to magic.

—Suzanne Finnamore, American author

I HAVE ALWAYS wanted to be a parent and have never doubted my desire to have children; it was always central to my being. I knew it was an important choice and that it was imperative to be responsible and unselfish. I was in awe of my daughters, loving them from the very first instant with a deep feeling of gratitude and joy. Both of my pregnancies had difficult moments, and I recognized that my children were a great gift.

You have been given a gift in the role of parent. You have the opportunity to foster other beings on their journeys, to watch them grow and develop, to honor their individuality, to give them room to explore, and to cheer their successes and lament their losses. This role comes with no manual, no tried and true way of approaching the situations you will encounter. You can consider the opinions of others, consult authorities, and read books on parenting techniques and philosophies, but in the end, you have to decide for yourself what is right for you and your child. Your choices will have a significant impact on your children's lives— and all who come into contact with them.

The essence of parenting is replete with opportunities to give unconditionally and act selflessly; there are many opportunities for both, and there are many times on a daily basis when you have to consider what is in the best interests of your child.

There are also infinite moments where you will experience pure, unfiltered love, compassion, and forgiveness. You will have the privilege of seeing the purity of a child's soul, treasuring the beauty in each moment, and giving your attention to what really matters. We have been given a great honor, but sometimes the depth of what we feel is frightening, the worry we face over things we cannot control is overwhelming, and the pain we feel when our children are hurting is devastating. Parenting also takes great courage; sometimes there are difficult decisions and unpopular choices to make. However, if our intentions are pure and our choices are based in love, all will work out.

A parent's job is to focus on the positive, to focus on what we love about our children and what they are doing right. This leads to moments that connect us to them and to who we truly are. We need to remember to enjoy our children in the moment, focusing only on what is important and discarding the rest. We need to cherish this gift daily, but even more so in the difficult times. Your children need your love the most when they act in unloving ways. They need your tolerance and patience when they are being difficult. They need you most when they push you away.

Sometimes our love is hard to give, and we have to work on moving past our own resistance to a place of compassion for our children. This place is beautiful because it is real and honest. Here, each of us is in touch with who we truly are. Here, we both experience a moment of grace.

There is no greater insight we can have than to gain an accurate awareness about the significance of the beautiful gift we have been given in the role of parent.

. . . .

Think of all the reasons you are grateful to be a parent. How has this experience shaped your life and the life of others? Tell your children during the next opportunity you have about all the reasons why you are grateful to be their parent.

. . . .

The Laundry Can Wait

*Breathe. Let go. And remind yourself that this very moment is
the only one you know you have for sure.*

—Oprah Winfrey, American media proprietor,
talk show host, actress, and producer

CHILDHOOD GOES BY in a flash; one day you will look back and
wonder where the time went. How did your children become
adults when it seems like just yesterday they were in diapers?
When your children are older, these memories seem precious,
but when your children are young, there are days that seem
endless and you long for the time when you will have more
independence. Remind yourself that those days will come, but
for now, it is more important to spend time with your children
than to worry about your to-do list or household chores. When
my girls were young, there were times I would become irritated
at the constant interruptions in my day; I was never able to finish
something I started. Now, I am grateful when my daughters
interrupt what I am doing to bring me into their lives.

Your children need your attention and your presence. They
need you to be with them, not just to be around. Children don't
look back with fondness and say their mom was awesome because
the laundry was always done or the house was spotless. They
won't say that their father was great because he never missed a
day of work. They need your attention; they need to know they
matter, and that they are a priority. Clean clothes and a semblance
of order in the home are important, but there is a balance here that
comes with letting go of perfection and making sure you spend

quality time with your children. You cannot get this time back later. They need the gift of you more than they need a big home, lavish vacations, or extravagant presents.

It is important to focus your attention on what is important and not to "sweat the small stuff." If your son wants to wear his Halloween costume to the store, let him. If your daughter doesn't want to ride the rollercoaster at the park, don't pressure her. If your son wants to play with dolls, it's okay. If you are late to a party because your children need your attention, so be it. When your daughter doesn't want to kiss Aunt Harriet good-bye, don't force her. Direct your efforts to what really matters, and let the insignificant matters go.

Spending time with your adolescent is just as important as with your toddler. Sometimes we have to be more flexible when children are older and meet them where they are comfortable. We might learn to play video games, horseback ride, or rollerblade. We could learn to cook or throw a softball. As long as you are connecting on some level, the time is well spent and will result in a closer bond in the future. It's important to remember that we are only given the gift of now and to be mindful of treasuring these experiences with our children.

As we focus on what we enjoy about each moment and what we can bring to it, we create the relationships we want with our children.

. . . .

Make it a point to spend quality time with your children at your next opportunity. Be fully present and focus on the interaction with your child. What did you learn from this experience that you may not have noticed before? What was your children's reaction to your time together?

. . . .

Obligations

We must be willing to let go of the life we have planned, so as to have the life that is waiting for us.

—Joseph Campbell, American
mythologist, writer, and lecturer

THERE ARE DAYS when parenting feels like a string of obligations. Chores, cooking, laundry, cleaning, and chauffeuring seem to pile up. When you are feeling overwhelmed, it is a signal that you need to take part in experiences that are reenergizing and relaxing. Making time for yourself is not selfish and does not mean you are neglecting your child. This time is crucial in order to have the internal resources for the demands of your role.

We don't want to view our parenting role as a duty instead of cherishing it. Our lives should be fun: a time to explore, grow, and most of all, experience joy, laughter, and love. Don't fall into the habit of taking anything too seriously, particularly your role as a parent.

When it feels as if we have lost the joy in everyday living, we need to remember the obligation we have to ourselves as well. We need to take care of ourselves by nurturing our souls, taking care of our health, and paying attention to what makes us happy. That could mean saying no to others or asking for help. It may involve setting boundaries regarding how you allocate your time. Perhaps the right decision for you is to be a working mother instead of a stay-at-home mother. Or you may decide to give up your career to be at home. You might need to schedule time for you and your partner, just as you schedule other important appointments. This is not wrong or selfish. You can look into sharing babysitting time with other parents. You can ask family members to help out or hire a mother's helper. There are inexpensive childcare programs that could be fun for your children while giving you some respite. There are always solutions if we are open to them.

Life as well as parenting can be fun, fulfilling, and joyful. We need balance, and we need to make ourselves a priority. We cannot give to our children when we are exhausted, or we will end up resenting them. Author Marcelene Cox noted, "Parents are often so busy with the physical rearing of children that they miss the glory of parenthood, just as the grandeur of the trees is lost while raking." So true.

Our minds, bodies, and spirits need time to unwind and recharge. Activity is fun and action is fine, but real learning occurs when we slow down and listen to the truth of our inner voices. We have been programmed to think inactivity is lazy and unproductive; we are a result-oriented society that devalues the benefits of slowing down. Sometimes we keep ourselves busy in order to avoid the introspection we sorely need. Don't deny yourself the time to stop and renew your energy. You deserve it, and you will be a better parent because of it.

Your children need unscheduled time as well. I have seen young children chauffeured from flute lessons to parties and to tutoring sessions with no time to decompress. Is that the life we intend for our children? How will their imaginations blossom? How will they know what they really like? I know that I become irritable when I am overscheduled, and it is the same for children.

I see students who race through their day as though they were running a marathon. They attend school and take a difficult curriculum, participate in myriad activities or grueling athletic programs, work part-time jobs and volunteer, complete homework, wake up at six, and do it all again. I can see the stress in their eyes and the tension in their faces, but they are not open to negotiating the demands of their days. There is fear in not measuring up, in disappointing, and in having to give thought to what they really want. That place creates anxiety for them.

These are the students who cannot make decisions for themselves, won't acknowledge what they want, or never smile.

Don't pressure your children or instill them with the fear of not being enough. Let them make choices based upon what makes them happy, not what they feel obligated to do. The key is to help them find and wholeheartedly pursue that which they love. They don't want to disappoint you, their coaches, or their teachers, but give them the courage to do so. Make sure they understand that they are allowed to disappoint others by being true to themselves.

Show your children that taking care of ourselves, physically and emotionally, is our first obligation and should always be honored.

Pick one obligation that you would like to let go of. Make a decision to no longer participate in this responsibility and state your intention to let it go. How does that feel to you? Examine the positive and negative feelings it brings up for you. Will you stick to your decision? What positive experience can take its place?

Honesty

Honesty: the best of all the lost arts.

—Mark Twain, American author and humorist

I RECALL A conversation with a parent who shared that her husband had recently been diagnosed with colon cancer. The parents decided they were not going to tell their teenage children because they didn't want them to be upset or to worry. Her husband was going to receive the full course of treatment for the disease without telling anyone about his illness.

Kids have a built-in lie detector and can smell a lie a mile away. They may not call you on it or be able to articulate why they feel that way, but they know when you are being evasive, making excuses, or just plain lying. Sometimes under the guise of protecting our children, we lie because it is easier. We may be embarrassed or just too tired to get into the important conversations that telling the truth often leads to. If you want your children to place stock in what you tell them, make the decision to be honest with them and be sure to keep your word.

When we are honest, we lay our faults and our frailties out on the table. We don't presume to be perfect, and this gives our children permission to accept themselves with their own faults. Our children are not shocked when they get out into the world and see the imperfections it holds because they have seen them in us. They learn that to be human means we make mistakes; at times, we are weak instead of strong, cruel instead of kind, and selfish instead of loving. Only when we acknowledge these imperfections can we move on to make better choices.

Think about the reasons why you might hold something back from your children. Are you afraid they wouldn't be able to handle the reality of the situation? Would it reveal more about you or a family member than you want to reveal? Be honest with yourself first. When you answer your children's questions genuinely, you are telling them you have confidence in their ability to handle the issues that life brings. You are letting them know you will be honest with them whenever possible and that you expect the same from them. If they catch you in a lie, how can you hold them accountable when they do the same?

This does not mean they need to know every detail of every situation, and there is some information that is not necessary for them to be exposed to. But when you withhold information that is truly important to them, they sense it; they know something is wrong and become anxious about what you are not telling them. Secrets have a way of getting out, and it is better that they hear the truth from you first.

While the truth is not always easy, it indicates that you are living life with integrity and authenticity. Our children are capable of understanding more about life than we give them credit for, and we need to examine the reasons we choose to withhold information.

Our children will grow up more equipped to handle the challenges that life brings if they are not sheltered from understanding how to approach these challenges at a young age.

. . . .

Consider a time when you were less than honest. How did this situation make you feel during and after the event? Would you make the same decision the next time?

. . . .

Children With Disabilities

I choose not to place the "dis" in my ability.

—Robert M. Hensel, Guinness World Record
holder and spokesperson for Athletes for Hope

TEN-YEAR-OLD MELISSA SHANG is currently petitioning the American Girl brand, a division of Mattel, to choose a doll with a disability as the 2015 American Girl of the Year because she wants to stress that disabled girls are American girls too. Her petition states, "For once, I don't want to be invisible or as a side character that the main American Girl has to help, I want other girls to know what it's like to be me, through a disabled American Girl's story. Disabled girls might be different from normal kids on the outside. They might sit in a wheelchair like I do, or have some other difficulty that other kids don't have. However, we are the same as the other girls on the inside, with the same thoughts and feelings. American Girls are supposed to represent all the girls that make up American history past and present and that includes disabled girls."

I have worked with children living with chronic illnesses or disabling conditions: children who are blind or deaf, who have cerebral palsy, Tourette's syndrome, Type I diabetes, or severe learning disabilities. In all cases, these children have made no excuses for their situations, regularly excelling without much fanfare. They are often surprised when asked about how they have handled adversity because their conditions have become commonplace, not a way of defining themselves.

I sit back in awe when I think about blind students who are able to navigate a large high school building on their own or when a student with Tourette's syndrome has the courage to give a speech in class. It is awe-inspiring when the student with cerebral palsy chooses to take the crowded stairway over the elevator. I admire their courage and that of their parents. This world can be a difficult place for a growing child, and when you add a disability into the mix, it is even more so. I have seen parents focusing on fostering independence and strength in their children with less coddling. The parents know they have to help their children develop strong skills to be able to navigate the challenges ahead.

Parents can advocate for their children in order to seek out resources and allies. However, it may be done without enabling their children or creating dependency. If your child has a disability, be careful of well-meaning sources that speak of limitations and boundaries. Help your child decide what is right for him or her and focus on your child's strengths. Let them know that anything is possible when people follow their hearts; remarkable accomplishments and medical miracles are documented throughout history.

Our lives are only defined by our own belief systems; don't let your children take no for answer. Help them instead to value the strengths that adversity has created and support them in their goals despite the obstacles that may appear. Don't let your fears become their fears. Have the courage to support your children and their dreams. Author and poet Maya Angelou said, "You may not control all the events that happen to you, but you can decide not to be reduced by them."

Shine the spotlight on your children's accomplishments, and they will accomplish even more.

• •

If your child has a disability, how do you view this? Consider the many ways you can encourage your children to reach for their dreams.

• •

An Open Door

The best way to keep children at home is to make the home atmosphere pleasant, and let the air out of the tires.

—Dorothy Parker, American poet, short-story writer, critic, and satirist

ALLOWING YOUR HOME to be a place for your children's friends to assemble has its benefits. It may be noisier and you may get less sleep, but you will learn who your children's friends are and you will get to know their parents as well. You may have to be more flexible, your house will not be as clean, and your food bill may increase, but you will know where your children are and what they are doing. You may also find that you have an extra plate at the dinner table for the child whose home is not as welcoming.

That being said, you do not have to allow behavior in your home that other parents allow in theirs. Some parents allow their teenagers to have coed sleepovers or drinking parties in their homes, saying that at least they know where their children are. That is a personal decision, but you have to consider the consequences if you can't fully supervise what is going on. Nonetheless, you are responsible for the behavior.

I remember when our daughter said our home was called "The Sober House" because we didn't allow her friends to drink here. It's not like we didn't have a drink in our home with our adult friends or that our older children couldn't have a drink with us when we had company. It just didn't feel right to us to sanction the activities in our house for our daughter's friends. I can't say what the right answer is for everyone; you have to do what feels right to you without any pressure from anyone else, particularly your children.

On one occasion, we acquiesced and allowed our daughter's friends to stay overnight and drink moderately. We were up all night, listening and monitoring, watching who left in the morning, and checking their condition before they drove home. It was not fun, and we worried all night. It didn't feel right to us, and it didn't happen again. But that did not stop my daughter's friends from coming here when they had problems at home or needed some help. The bottom line is that you have to do what feels right when it comes to welcoming your children's friends into your home, and there are benefits to letting your home be the house they feel comfortable to visit within those parameters.

It is important to extend that option to your children as well, even after they are on their own. Our world can be challenging at times, consisting of unfair events, difficult experiences, and disappointments. As your children grow older, your home should provide a soft place to land. It should be a place where your children can get themselves together without judgment, a faultfinding mission, or a lecture. Depending upon your children's temperament, they may just need some solitude and acceptance. Give them space, pick up on the cues they are giving, and be patient. Let them navigate this process in the manner that is best for them.

Be the one your children can come to in times of trouble because there will be times of trouble, even for the most easygoing child. There will be occasions when a relationship breakup is difficult, they lose their jobs, or they get knocked around in the world. This does not mean that encouraging your thirty-five year-old to live in your home to escape the responsibilities of the real world is warranted. Each situation is unique, and it is important to ask yourself what is truly best for your children at that time.

Let your home have an open door for your children, and let it be the place they can come to for solace.

· ·

Have a discussion with your partner and children about the expectations of having your children's friends in your home. What are your boundaries? What is acceptable, and what is not?

How would feel if your grown child needed to come home after a difficult experience? Consider how the open door policy would work in your home.

· ·

When A Child Is Ill

With the new day comes new strength and new thoughts.

—Eleanor Roosevelt, longest-serving
First Lady of the United States

THE ISSUES INVOLVED in parenting can be overwhelming, but they pale in comparison to the difficulties that arise when a child is seriously ill. The typical worries associated with parenting are overshadowed by serious concerns about health and safety. It is crucial for the parents of a child who is ill to have logistical support for the responsibilities of everyday living as well as emotional support for what they are going through. Contacting those experiencing similar issues—and support from friends, family, and school staff—can be helpful.

I have witnessed families dealing with myriad illnesses, including childhood cancer, and I am amazed at their strength and fortitude. I am sure there are times when the resolve is not so strong and fear takes hold. But in many cases, I see gratitude for the medical milestones and increased solidarity within the families.

There are times when we wonder why these illnesses occur at all, particularly to children. It seems so unfair. That concept has always been difficult for me to understand. Although I don't practice religion in the traditional sense, I do believe there is a power that created us—that we are a part of a loving energy that connects us to each other. I have often wondered how the God I believe in could allow these tragedies to happen, the illnesses, diseases, accidents, natural disasters, and the violence we perpetrate upon each other. I could never reconcile these events in my mind with the loving God I envisioned, particularly when children were involved.

Beneath the illusion of our everyday reality, we are perfect, immortal beings having mortal experiences. We may have had hundreds or even thousands of prior lifetimes with eternity ahead of us. French Enlightenment philosopher Voltaire wrote, "It is not surprising to be born twice more than once, everything in nature is resurrection."

Perhaps the reasons for these difficult experiences are to foster our soul's growth, to help us define who we are, and to allow us to experience diverse aspects of life. As difficult as it is to imagine, this adversity can motivate us to make greater contributions to society than we would have otherwise and our purpose is always connected to the experience of love, for ourselves and for others. If we consider that the soul is housed in a particular body in a lifetime for a purpose, we understand that these are not random occurrences. It may provide some comfort, and it might give an explanation to the question of why these events occur—why a child is ill or has a disability.

Tina entered eleventh grade after being diagnosed with schizophrenia the year before. She was a gentle young woman, with eyes full of kindness and promise. Her mother was a staunch advocate for her needs, always there to support her and to pave the way. She was receiving treatment outside of school as well as support in school, and all was going well. She was a good student, had friends, and things were manageable. Tina graduated and was accepted to college.

Several years later, Tina's mother called to see if I would meet with them. She said Tina was living on the street, had been arrested for shoplifting, and was in trouble. She thought I might be able to connect with her and provide direction since we had a good relationship. I was taken aback when I saw Tina; her eyes were hard, and her demeanor had a tough edge to it. She was going through a very difficult time. I admire Tina's mother greatly as she continued to advocate for her daughter through the different stages of illness, even when her dreams for her daughter did not come to fruition. I admire Tina as well, trying to deal with an illness that can be very difficult to manage.

I know there is meaning to Tina's experience, but I am not sure what it is. Perhaps it is to gain compassion for those who are struggling with mental illness or empathy for those in trouble. It was heartbreaking to see, and I can only imagine what they have gone through. I witnessed as Tina's mom continued to advocate for her, and if her mission was to support her child through all of her challenges, she fulfilled it with grace.

Sometimes we can see the reasons and the meaning behind the events that we go through, and sometimes, as in the case of Tina, it is not readily apparent.

Things happen for a reason and in time, whether in this lifetime or not, everything will make sense.

· ·

Be grateful for every day with your children, for the wonderful moments as well as the difficult ones, for the good times and the challenging times. Revel in the milestones and the triumphs, have faith, and remain hopeful in the hard times. Keep everything in perspective, knowing that we only have this moment to cherish.

· ·

Friendship

Walking with a friend in the dark is better than walking alone in the light.

—Helen Keller, American author,
political activist, and lecturer

YOUR CHILDREN NEED you to fulfill the role of parent, first and foremost. At times, parents believe that being their children's friend is more important than assuming the unpopular role of a parent who sets limits and accepts responsibility, but that is a mistake. When we give our children too much freedom with no boundaries, they experience anxiety at the power they have been prematurely given—and they will not use it wisely.

My friend was in the midst of a divorce; she decided she wanted to start a new life as her marriage of many years had disintegrated. Events surrounding the divorce became acrimonious for all, and she felt very guilty about the effect it was having on her children. My friend began to bribe her children with extravagant gifts and outings, attempting to garner their favor and compensate for her feelings of guilt. The children were given anything they wanted and could do anything they wanted, regardless of their behavior.

Young children and teenagers need reasonable boundaries, stability, and consistency. They feel secure when you create structure for them because they are not ready for so much freedom; it makes them feel nervous and abandoned. When you try to be your children's friend before being a parent, it usually is because you are trying to earn their approval or you are feeling guilty. You give in when you should say no or let them make decisions they are not ready for. You give them whatever they want without letting them earn anything. While it appears they are happy with this arrangement, it a false happiness. It stems from guilt or fear, certainly not from love.

Your relationship will progress and evolve. Perhaps you will be friends in the future, but while your children are growing, it is essential that they know how to establish sound friendships with their peers. Building friendships is an important skill for your children to learn. You can help your children understand that friends can encourage each other to grow without imposing their values on each other. They will share laughs and dreams, but they will also support each other in times of need. Friends tell you the truth when it counts, even though it is hard to do. Friends may not be able to spare you the pain of heartbreak or change difficult circumstances, but they will get down in the trenches with you when they occur. Help your children understand what a gift true friendship is, and let them know that they have to *be* true friends to *have* true friends.

I have worked with a number of students over the years that were having difficulty maintaining friendships. I have seen girls so eager to have friends that they chose the first people who approached them without deciding if these were friendships they really wanted; consequently, they often found the relationships unsatisfying. I have seen boys continue friendships out of obligation long after they outgrew the relationships. I have seen students so used to getting their own way at home that they did not know that friendships are comprised of compromise, empathy, and altruism. As a result, they were never able to sustain the friendships they initiated.

Encourage your children to practice the skills it takes to be and keep a good friend, such as compromise, honesty, tact, good listening skills, and reliability. Help them strengthen these skills within your family system; you can model these skills for them at home. Help your children realize that a good friend is invaluable and that some relationships blossom quickly while others take time to nurture. Some friendships are long lasting, and some are fleeting, but they all teach us something about ourselves.

The relationships we enter into are not random or haphazard. They are presented to help us grow, to teach us something we need to learn, and to help us define our preferences. These relationships are arranged for us because they offer the greatest potential for growth. They benefit both parties and provide a forum for development, expansion of new skills, and an avenue to obtain the knowledge we need. Our relationships serve as a mirror for us, reflecting our beliefs about ourselves and the way we view the world.

Help your children learn from these relationships and appreciate what they have learned, even when the relationship was painful. There is a lesson in these experiences for all of us, no matter our ages.

Do not orchestrate relationships for your child. These are growth opportunities, and your children need to experience this phase of development for themselves.

. . . .

Let your children choose their friends based on who they feel comfortable with, who they respect and who respects them, whose company they enjoy, and who makes them laugh. Let them learn from the lessons these relationships teach them.

Think of your own friendships. What have you learned from them? What have you brought to your relationships?

. . . .

Forgiveness

Forgiveness is almost a selfish act because of its immense benefits to the one who forgives.

—Lawana Blackwell, American writer

PARENTING CAN BE the most wonderful experience as well as the hardest thing you ever go through. It can push you to your breaking point while giving you experiences that bring the greatest joy imaginable. But there will be times when you stumble and fall, when you act in a way you regret, or when you are ashamed of the words that tumble out of your mouth. You need to give yourself a break and learn from your mistakes to improve the future, while also realizing you only have the present to act upon now. Being mired in regret will only lead to actions stemming from guilt and fear, which are never productive for you or your children.

There have been moments where I looked back and felt regret at some of the words I said. There were choices I made that I would change if I could. There are decisions I made that I would not make now. I cannot take back those choices, but I can work on being a better parent now because no matter how old your children are, every parent-child relationship can grow and improve. When you learn to forgive yourself for the flaws in your parenting, you may find that you now have the capacity to forgive others more easily, including your own parents. You come to understand that parenting is no easy task.

It is a cruel trick our mind plays on us: flashbacks of times when we could have made different choices, said different things, stood up for someone, or taken advantage of opportunities. Many times, we seem to replay only our failures. Our minds introduce worries about the future, living there instead of here where our power is. My yoga instructor calls it our "endless monkey-mind chatter." Our life only exists in the present; the past and the future do not exist here unless we bring them along.

We have to realize that we have control over our minds. It is a tool, but it is not who we are. Our minds are waiting for us to take the reins. But like children, if we do not, it will. We can use them to create what we want in our lives and to be the parents and people we want to be. If we let our minds run wild, we will look back and wonder why our lives turned out in ways we didn't want.

Forgiveness occurs when you are at peace with yourself despite all other circumstances. Your ego rallies for you to hold onto your feelings of disappointment or anger because it takes pride in being right, no matter the cost. It derives power from our indecision and insecurity. But our truth lies in letting go of this control and accepting what is, rather than what was or what could be. When we forgive the imperfections in ourselves, we are able to forgive them more easily in others.

As my children have grown, I asked myself if I did everything I could when they were young to help them flourish. Although I did my best, the honest answer is no. I would make some of the same choices, but I would also do some things differently. But I am only capable of saying this now because I have gained wisdom I did not have then.

Have patience with yourself, and the practice of acceptance. While it is a simple concept, it is not always an easy one.

When you move into forgiveness of your own faults, you will experience true peace.

For what reasons are you not granting forgiveness to yourself? Look at those areas to see where you can grant compassion. Can you choose to forgive yourself, knowing that you did your best at the time? Make a list of all the things you have learned and the ways you have grown.

Money

Money is only a tool. It will take you wherever you wish, but it will not replace you as the driver.

—Ayn Rand, American novelist, philosopher, playwright, and songwriter

My HUSBAND WITNESSED something interesting while traveling on the ferry one day. An elderly woman, supporting herself with a cane in each hand, walked painstakingly slowly and deliberately toward the elevator. Quite suddenly, she looked down and stopped. My husband was about to go over to see if she needed help, when rather abruptly and with lightning speed, she put her canes down on the seat next to her. Then she stooped over to pick up a penny on the floor. She put the penny in her pocketbook, repositioned her canes, and made her way slowly to her destination.

Money is very important to us. We give it more power than any other type of energy. And money is just that—another form of energy we interact with. We give money a lot of influence over how we live our lives. We give it the power to make us happy or miserable. We believe it gives us the freedom to live our lives as we choose. We let it determine our self-worth, and we judge others because of it. Money creates conflicting feelings. We are happy when we have it, sad when we don't.

We need to examine our views toward money so we can help our children establish authentic relationships with it. If our children hear us complain about the lack of money in our lives or watch how upset we become when discussing money, it will not set a good example for them. Take a look at your relationship with this form of energy. Look at the environment you grew up in to see if you are continuing patterns that do not serve your family.

There are many prevalent attitudes about money that can actually prevent it from coming into your life. Erroneously, we believe that money can only come from hard work, that money is the root of all evil, or that it is not virtuous to desire money. We believe that having money changes people or that there is not enough money to go around. Too often, people believe some of these theories, and this will keep money at a distance.

Others believe they can only be happy, free, or enjoy their lives if they have money. However, what we may not realize is that we are already wealthy; money does not equate to wealth. Wealth stems from recognizing all the gifts we have been given. We have a choice about what we feel, and we can choose happiness just like we choose an outfit for the day. In fact, being happy, loving, and joyful will draw money to us because our energy and vibration are now set at a much higher level.

When we say we don't have enough money, we send out a signal to the universe that states we are not prosperous and that signal will bring us experiences that match this vibration. As stated by Abraham of Abraham-Hicks, "Whatever I am looking at, I am including in my vibration." This vibration, positive or negative, is sent out into the universe and draws corresponding experiences to our lives. Even if our finances could use improvement, focusing on areas in our lives that are abundant— jobs we enjoy, loving relationships, great friendships, or good health—will bring us additional events to be grateful for, including improvement in our finances.

Those are just some examples of a mindset that will set up a relationship with money that is inaccurate at best and damaging at the worst. These beliefs can lead to a life of struggle when it is not necessary. The truth is that we are all deserving of living an abundant, prosperous lifestyle. Doing so gives us the time and energy to focus on our gifts and talents. We have to remember that we get what we think we deserve. Our experiences match the energy we exude, what we embody, and what we think, believe, and feel. Money fits perfectly into this equation.

We get what we give out; there is no way around this. If we are selfish and miserly with our love, time, or attention, this form of lack will return to us in some way. If we take love from others without returning it, cheat others, or take what does not belong to us, this will show up in our lives somewhere as a form of scarcity. The universe is not punitive, but it is always fair and is always seeking balance. If we give love to others, it will return to us multiplied. If we are generous and give from our hearts, we will receive much more in return. If we are selfish or cruel, something will be taken from us.

> *"Life is an echo. What you send out, comes back. What you sow, you reap. What you give, you get. What you see in others exists in you."*
>
> —Hilary Hinton "Zig" Ziglar, American author, salesman, and motivational speaker.

It is important that our children understand these laws so they can create what they want in their lives with purpose. It's important to teach our children to appreciate and respect money, to manage money responsibly, and to understand it is our inherent birthright to live lives that are filled with prosperity of all kinds. This includes financial abundance, perfect health, fulfilling relationships, careers we enjoy, and lives of purpose and vision.

A life filled with all forms of abundance is available if you believe you deserve it—and if you choose to allow it in.

What is your relationship with money? Do you lack the money you would like in your life? If so, examine where the discrepancy lies. Where are you not aligned with the truth? What do you discover when you examine these beliefs and evaluate them?

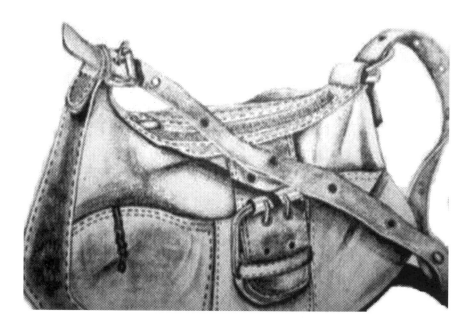

In The Case of Divorce

Storms make trees grow stronger.

—Dolly Parton, American singer-songwriter,
actor, author, and philanthropist

A DIVORCE CAN be painful for a child of any age, and no matter how amicable the terms, it shakes the very foundation of a child's world. The child's family system is changing, and the two most important people to the child are parting. There are often feelings of guilt, anger, resentment, and confusion.

Divorce may be the best option for the family, but a mistake I see parents make is subjecting the children to adversarial comments or unkind actions directed toward the other parent. This is pure selfishness, and it is devastating for the child, even when there is truth behind those words. It forces the child to align with one parent at a time and makes the event much more difficult for all involved. Parents need to demonstrate maturity and insight. They need to put their own feelings aside, deal with them in the appropriate setting, and realize they are hurting their children tremendously when they behave in that manner.

Parents who are divorcing have created a child together, once born out of love. Let that love at least turn into fairness, tolerance, and acceptance. Let your children know you will be there for them, that you will love them always, and that the divorce was not their fault by any means. Work together to raise and support this life you brought into the world. Show your children that hurting others, even when you are hurting, is never a good choice. This is the greatest gift you can give your children in this difficult circumstance.

I have witnessed how families of divorce cope with co-parenting on many occasions in my office. There have been times when I could not believe the behavior that was taking place. I have seen situations when a lawyer needed to mediate every interchange between the parents about their children. I have been in parent-child conferences where the barbs and remarks that were thrown back and forth in front of the child were horrific as the child sat there, like a pawn in a chess game.

I have also witnessed harmonious situations where the parents cooperatively raised their children by demonstrating maturity and responsibility.

Children benefit immensely when parents co-parent wisely, and as a result, their children can deal with the ramifications of the divorce from a stronger, much more secure place.

· ·

If you are involved in a divorce, work with your ex-partner to create an amicable, working relationship. That is a wonderful gift to give your child. If it seems impossible, remember that only you have control over how you behave, what you say, and what you share with your child. What you choose in this situation has great consequences.

· ·

They Want Your Attention

The most precious gift we can offer anyone is our attention. When mindfulness embraces those we love, they will bloom like flowers.

—Thich Nhat Hanh, Vietnamese Zen Buddhist monk, teacher, author, and peace activist

YOUR CHILDREN WANT your attention. This is readily apparent when children are young and love to be around their parents. This desire does not fade away as children grow; it just changes form, and we need to maintain these connections with our children as they enter the teenage years and beyond. Children have a need for privacy, and that is to be respected. However, they still desperately need to spend time with you. There is a middle ground here, a place where you can give your children the room to become independent young adults, while remaining connected and close.

I have spoken with children who feel unwanted and abandoned by parents pursuing their own social lives and careers while neglecting time with them at home. These children are the last ones you would except to hear this from. They are often the ones who are involved in behaviors that place them at risk and are usually in some type of trouble. However, underneath their gruff exteriors, they just want love and attention from their parents. If their families are not meeting those needs, they will look elsewhere to fill the void.

No matter how disagreeable or difficult your children are, know that they still need and want you. Sometimes, in this situation, your love may be more difficult for them to accept or for you to give. These children need you to move past any disappointments you may have in them. Don't accept their disrespect, but don't take it personally either. Focus your attention on what you love about them.

Growing children are seeking consistency and stability, things they can count on in their rapidly changing worlds. Have dinner together and talk about the day, make plans to do something they enjoy, keep them connected to the extended family, continue family traditions, and enjoy spending time together in any form.

Make plans to devote time to your children, no matter how much they protest, knowing deep down that they want and need that connection with you.

• •

Be aware of a time when your children needed your attention. Were you present? Did you fill that need?

This week, take the opportunity to give your full attention to your children. Be aware of the impact on your interaction. Be cognizant of experiences in the future that will help your children feel valued, no matter their ages.

• •

Love Without Condition

If people are going to be allowed to say "We love you" and "I love you," they'd better have the backbone to prove it. Love isn't just a word.

—C. JoyBell C., poet, essayist, novelist, and author

IMAGINE THE WONDERFUL things that would take place if we loved ourselves—and others—unconditionally. Imagine if we loved our children without strings attached—without expectations, neediness, or conditions upon which our love would be bestowed. What if our happiness did not depend upon our children's actions or successes? We would love them and be loved in return because of whom we both truly are and just because we exist. How freeing that would be, for us and for them.

It is a simplistic concept, yet hard to envision as a practice. Often, we expect our children to meet our needs and make us happy. This places a burden on them and perpetuates the falsehood that others are in charge of our happiness and peace of mind. When we navigate the world in this manner, we give our power away.

Like many concepts in this book, the practice of unconditional love has been a work-in-progress for me. I can look back and see where I have not been pleased about some choices my daughters have made. This is because I am taking things too personally, looking at them as reflections of me, and not respecting that my children are separate entities. At times, I have let their actions dictate my happiness, and that has not been good for any of us.

Throughout the phases of our children's lives, we may want them to be something they are not. We want them to act in particular manners or make certain choices in order to meet our own needs. We may have some judgment about the way they behave, whether spoken or not. Perhaps we want our little boy to be an athlete except he wants to read all the time or we worry because our little girl is so outspoken and assertive. As they become teenagers and young adults, our children may make choices that offend or embarrass us.

We need to understand that our children are not replicas of us, and they are not responsible for how we see ourselves. We can choose to take the blame or the credit for their actions, but that is a false reality.

If we teach our children that they are not dependent upon people or circumstances to make them happy, we would give them a head start in navigating the world. The best way we can demonstrate this is through unconditional love, even when we don't approve of their behavior. We can separate our children's actions from who they are. We can also choose to be happy when they do something to upset us or when circumstances don't work out as we like. We are the role models for our children, demonstrating that our power rests inside of us. By loving ourselves, we honor that power.

Unconditional love is not indecisive. It is not weak; it is not fragile. It does not look away and smile when a child is being rude to others; it does not give in when the child is having a tantrum. It does not enable the child who is in trouble or make excuses for a child who needs to learn accountability. Unconditional love cherishes the child beneath the actions, but it does not ignore behavior that is incorrect. This type of love honors the child enough to use each experience as an opportunity to encourage self-growth.

Love is truly what we are all seeking—love for ourselves and love for others. There is nothing to take its place, and nothing will fill the void—not money, not power, not fame. Love is all that remains when the illusion of pain and separation vanish.

Profound love for those in our lives can lead to the transformation of our relationships. Self-love leads to the transformation of our own lives. Unconditional love for others and ourselves will transform the world.

Love for our children occurs when we view their dark sides with acceptance; we observe their wounds and their scars, but we love them regardless, knowing that we have a shadow side as well. We offer love because of who they are underneath all that life has shown them; knowing we are all perfect just as we are and we are all doing our best.

Ultimately, we are responsible for our own happiness and so are our children, no matter their ages.

If we lived our lives by practicing unconditional love, we would see miraculous changes in our relationships with others, but most of all in the way we view our lives on a daily basis.

Take the opportunity to demonstrate unconditional love for someone in your life, particularly when it is not easy to do so. What chord does this strike within you? Was it easy to do? Difficult? Impossible?

Consider how it makes you feel when are able to demonstrate love without expecting something in return. Does it make you feel weak or strong? Vulnerable or powerful? In or out of control?

Parenting Adult Children

You'll love your children far more than you ever loved your parents—and in the recognition that your own children cannot fathom the depth of your love—you come to understand the tragic, unrequited love of your own parents.

—Ursula Hegi, German-born American writer

I HAVE SPOKEN to a number of parents, both professionally and privately, who have shared that if they had to choose whether or not to have children over again, it would give them pause. Some have shared that they would choose not to. I am referring to wonderful, caring people who have dedicated their lives to raising their children. They are unselfish, loving, responsible people who are now experiencing profound sadness. They are feeling pain and disappointment about the lack of return they are receiving for their years of sacrifice and contribution. It saddens me to hear that, but I can say honestly say that on a fleeting occasion, I have felt that way as well.

Why is it that when our children become older and less dependent upon us, that we feel this way? Are we threatened by our children's independence, their unwillingness to share aspects of their lives with us, or our inability to receive a demonstration of unconditional love from them? Where is the disconnect, and why are parents feeling removed from their adult children's lives? I don't know all the answers, but perhaps we can entertain the notion that we are too dependent upon our children for fulfilling our sense of happiness. Do we need them to make up for what we lack in our lives, whether it is love, inspiration, or purpose? Are we looking to our children to give our lives meaning, when at this juncture of our lives, we need to find this meaning for ourselves? I am certain that when we look to them, it places a burden they will avoid at all costs.

I wrote in an earlier section that we cannot love our children too much; however, we can love our children too much if it is not real, if it is really just fear masquerading behind love's curtain. We have to revisit that concept at this point in our lives to see if the love we are looking for from our children is something else. Maybe it is based on our own neediness, feelings of desperation, the need for control, or a feeling of incompleteness in our own lives.

At the point when our children are beginning lives of their own, we have more time to take stock of our own lives. We assess our accomplishments and our purpose. If we put all of our eggs in one basket and look only to the role of parent to fulfill our sense of purpose, we may now have to look deeper and do some soul-searching to find out what else life holds for us. That may bring some discomfort because the space that now exists wants to be filled. But change is good. It is healthy, and wonderful surprises may be in store if we are open to them. However, it could mean that a change of perception is in order. *We may have to find a place of more acceptance and less expectation in our relationships with our grown children.*

As we redefine ourselves, so do they. Our adult children are venturing out into the world and making decisions they can own. They are finding out who they are apart from us. If you think about it, we are doing the same thing. We have the time now to focus upon ourselves, to do what we choose, and to make decisions without considering how they will affect them first. As your children see you living your life with passion and purpose, they will respect that and will want to spend time with you. It will not be out of obligation, but out of a true desire to be with someone who is genuine, interesting, and finds life fun and fulfilling. They will be happy to seek out the company of someone who does not depend upon them for their happiness.

All relationships are comprised of energy, and this one is no different. Our power lies with changing our perceptions and not assuming the role of victim. If you are focusing upon what is lacking in your relationship, replaying arguments or harsh words, reviewing unkind actions or misdeeds, you will only receive more of the same.

We attract what we focus upon. We get what we think we can have. We bring to our lives what we think about.

You can change the relationship with your adult children by changing yourself. Give your attention to only what you love about your children. Focus on good memories and envision everything your relationship could become while you spend time enjoying your life. Find the time now to do the things, both large and small, that make you happy and bring you joy.

When you do, you will find that healthier, more authentic relationships with your children now have the space to emerge.

. . . .

Accept your adult children for who they are by letting go of who you wish they were.

. . . .

The Many Faces Of Family

*If you look deeply into the palm of your hand, you will see your
parents and all generations of your ancestors. All of them are
alive in this moment. Each is present in your body. You are the
continuation of each of these people.*

—Thich Nhat Hanh, Vietnamese Buddhist monk,
teacher, author, poet, and peace activist

THE TRADITIONAL NOTION of a family consisting of a mother,
father, and children has changed to encompass more variety. A
family might contain grandparents, same-sex parents, an aunt
or uncle, single parent, adoptive, or foster families, families of
divorce, stepparents, etc. There is no uniform definition, but a
family does consist of individuals who love and support each other
and have made a commitment to raising their children together.

Family is not determined by gender, sexual orientation, age,
or relationship; it is determined by love, dedication, support,
and purpose. If your children come from the traditional type of
family, help them view other types of families with understanding
and respect. It is important that you model this behavior as well.
If your children come from a non-traditional family, instill a sense
of pride in them and help them gain insight into the differences.
Help them find a way to explain these differences to others in a
way that feels comfortable to them.

There is not a specific type of family system that is better
than another as long as the basis is love and the intention is to
raise secure, loving, and joyful children. But within each of these
systems, it serves us to look at patterns that are passed down

from generation to generation. These stories, expectations, and customs are often passed on from parent to child, and they can shape our lives in ways we do not want if we are not aware of them. Some negative patterns that come to mind are addiction, obesity, poverty, and child abuse. Other are more subtle: punitive discipline instead of loving structure, an authoritarian approach rather than fair guidelines, the need to work tirelessly and the need for success above the enjoyment of the flow of life.

In an earlier section, I discussed the type of parent my father was and examined his shortcomings. I also discussed how he had the resolve to change a dysfunctional generational pattern that existed in his family, that of the neglect and abuse of children. Although I could choose to view his choices under the lens of poor parenting, I choose instead to be grateful he did not continue patterns that could have been even more damaging.

You are the one who can alter these patterns and create change for your family. You are the one who can make things better for your grandchildren and their children. Consider the child who comes from a long line of physicians but whose heart aches for artistic expression. Why shouldn't this child be encouraged to pursue his or her passion rather than continuing the family tradition? Think of the family that comes from a background of impoverishment. Can one parent break this cycle, perhaps through securing an education that will lead to greater opportunities?

If a parent could look beyond what has become a negative pattern for his or her family and resolve to make a change, it would be a wonderful gift for generations to come. It only takes one parent with the courage and desire to want more for himself or herself and the children to foster positive change within the family.

Look at the generational patterns within your family, even the subtle ones, and discard what does not serve to create new opportunities and new choices.

Think of the ways your family differs from the average family. How has that affected your children? What strengths have they developed? What patterns have been passed down through the generations? Is there a pattern you would like to change? Consider some ways this could be accomplished and resolve to take the first step.

Your Children Have
Their Own Paths

There are no extra pieces in the universe. Everyone is here because he or she has a place to fill and every piece must fit itself into the big jigsaw puzzle.

—Deepak Chopra, holistic physician and
alternative medicine practitioner

As PARENTS, WE want to protect our children from the negative experiences of the world. We direct their lives because we know what is best for them. We tell ourselves this is for the safety and benefit of our children, but I have learned that it generally serves our own needs.

Although it is painful to see them struggle, we need to understand that our children have their own journeys to make. It's difficult when we see our children make choices we don't agree with or that we feel may be harmful to them. But this is not our path; it is theirs, and sometimes we just have to watch and see how it all unfolds. This journey could be full of turbulent times or smooth sailing, but it belongs to our children and no one else.

All of us yearn to experience life on our own terms. People silence the messages from their inner selves with apathy, constant activity, hopelessness, or denial. Your children are here to connect with their inner selves and experience growth and fulfillment. Look at your children and imagine what their lessons might be in this lifetime. Where do they need to learn and grow? Where do their struggles take place? In what areas do they excel naturally and consistently make contributions?

We can't learn their lessons for our children, and we can't orchestrate their paths because we want to save them from the pain and indecision that accompanies growth. We cannot experience for them what they need to go through; if we do, the benefits of the lessons will not be theirs.

A Zen proverb says, "The obstacle is the path." What we encounter in life that is difficult for us holds hidden gems. We have been given these obstacles as a gift in order to foster our growth, and if we choose to view them that way, they may be less painful. Occasionally, the more we need to grow, the more difficult the lessons might be.

I have spoken with parents whose children have walked the path of addiction. This is a difficult, turbulent journey that provides no clear resolution. I have watched how this addiction has turned their lives upside down and how hard it is for the parent to remember the child that once was. There are times when walking away has been the best choice; any other would have enabled the addiction. On other occasions, holding out a hand was what was needed. This path, although painful, is not one the parent can choose to orchestrate. The child must make the decision to accept help. Sometimes, experiencing pain is the only thing that will help the child face the reality of what is happening, and it is agonizing to watch. There comes a point where the parent has to realize that this path is the child's unique path—and the parent is not in control. The parent can always send love to the child obscured behind the addiction, while remembering to practice self-love at the same time.

We have not entered into this lifetime to have everything we desire dropped at our feet. That is not a situation that would encourage our evolution; a life without any scars is clearly not one that would foster our growth. Picture a time when you have gone through a difficult experience and try to think of what you learned as a result. If a well-meaning individual shielded you from that experience, would you have learned what you needed to? There are no coincidences in our lives, and we are given precisely what we need at the time we need it, but because we have free will, we can choose whether to learn from these experiences.

Don't deprive your children of their lessons; you can't do their work for them. Whether they take place in the circumstances surrounding a learning disability, chronic illness, addiction, or financial hardship, they have been provided to help your children grow. You can support, guide, and give your children opportunities based in love, but you should not try to live their lives for them or shield them from the growth that living their lives will bring.

Our relationships with our children need to come from a place of love, unconditional acceptance, and freedom of choice. When our intentions come from this place, we separate our lives from theirs, and we find that our relationships with our children are much healthier.

As a result, we enjoy our own lives with much more joy and freedom.

· ·

Write down five things you notice about what your children's path might be. Why do you think they are here at this place and time? What are their lessons? How do you fit into this plan?

· ·

Your Future Relationship

Children begin by loving their parents; as they grow older, they judge them; sometimes they forgive them.

—Oscar Wilde, Irish writer and poet

AS YOUR CHILDREN grow, it is important to honor and respect the differences that each new stage brings. This relationship begins with complete dependence upon the parent and evolves to one where two adults desire to forge an equitable relationship. It may evolve yet again to dependence of the parent upon the child.

Each stage involves flexibility, patience, and empathy. Along the way, there are frequent shifts in the balance of power and decision-making. While children are young, it becomes easy for the parent to assume they know what is right and that their decision is always correct. However, this is a shortsighted approach. It is important to respect the process and the increasing independence of your children and not feel threatened by it. We need to recognize that, even at a young age, our children know what is right for them. It is important to demonstrate respect when your children's desires contrast with your own. We have to take our own egos out of the picture and realize our children are a separate entity with their own journeys.

Honor the journey and be grateful to be an important part of it, but know that your ultimate goal is your child's happiness and emotional independence. We all want our children to be strong and resilient, to at least be able to make choices even if they turn out to be "wrong" in the future. We want our relationship with our children to be built on trust, respect, and appreciation for each other's differences. This does not mean that you give in to your children's every whim because you are afraid they will not love you. This is not a relationship built on love, but one built on fear. But if you conduct your parenting approach in an authoritative dictatorship, you will encounter difficulty later on when your children rebels and does not respect you.

There is a balance that you are seeking of mutual respect—not of one who dictates and one who must obey. If you choose the latter, your future relationship is likely to be comprised of obligation and duty on the part of your children, or it may even be non-existent. There will be a time when your children choose to see you, have relationships with you, and let you become a part of their own families in the future.

I have witnessed far too many families where the members become estranged, and it is not a healthy situation for anyone.

Remember that you are building your future relationship with each choice you make, each word you speak, and each action you take.

. . . .

Envision your future relationship with your child. What would you want it to consist of? How do you want the relationship to develop? Think of ways you can foster the relationship you desire, and resolve to implement some of the ways.

. . . .

Is It Okay To Get A B?

To live is the rarest thing in the world. Most people exist, that is all.

—Oscar Wilde, Irish writer and poet

I DECIDED TO initiate a group-counseling program at my high school with another counselor. We ran successful groups in the past, and this time, we decided to target overachievers who were leading stressful existences. In the competitive district in which we worked, we knew there would be many students who could benefit from this type of group.

We advertised our proposed group, "It's Okay to Get a B" and spoke to students we thought could benefit from it. A funny thing happened. No one came to our meeting; we had no takers. In retrospect, it is not surprising. The students who were in need of this group were terrified at the concept we were proposing. The idea of producing less than perfection was counterintuitive to the tightly constructed lives they were living. I see students such as these fairly often, and I see them strongly connected to notions that are incorrect. They believe their self-worth is measured by statistics and achievements. These are the girls who turn to anorexia or self-injury to exert control over some facet of their lives when the pressure builds. These are the young men who don't slow down long enough to admit they have feelings and choices.

Please do not frighten your children with beliefs that will do them harm. We have to let our children breathe. We have to give them space. We have to let them choose what makes them happy.

We cannot place our goals and desires onto them to fulfill. We cannot measure our self-worth by their accolades. We cannot try to control them because our lives are out of control.

They will have options. They will get into colleges if they choose, and they will be successful, if they want to be. The most satisfying feeling in life is knowing we lived it by our rules, met our own goals, and pursued experiences that made us happy. If we train our children to live by others' standards and to look outside themselves for validation, we do them no favors. We can't give them the impression, whether spoken or implied, that their self-worth and our love depends upon their achievements.

Help your children know that they are deserving and loveable just because they are—no other reason is necessary.

. . . .

Let go of any preconceived notions you have about your children's success. Know that everything works out as planned and that your children are perfect just as they are. Let go of expectations and worries. Focus your intention on loving your children just as they are.

. . . .

Life Brings Us Who We Are

All the Powers in the Universe are already ours. It is we who have put our hands before our eyes and cry that it is dark.

—Swami Vive Kenanda, Indian Hindu monk

PARENTAL DECISION-MAKING IS largely generated from a place of worry. We make certain choices and prohibit others because we feel this will increase our children's level of safety and success in this world. There is merit to this; basic needs and safety measures have to be addressed, but often, we go too far. What we need to understand is that our lives—and our children's lives—are reflections of our inner states of mind and what we believe. We have more control over the inner and outer facets of our experiences than we realize. If we claimed ownership of this awareness, we would understand that the world we experience shows up precisely in the manner that it does because it is a vibrational match to our personal belief system.

Everything is energy, even the most solid objects or systems. All throughout the day, we give off energy and attract experiences that match it. For example, if you are feeling bad about yourself and remain in this place of self-deprecation for some time, you will attract an experience that mirrors that way of thinking. You may have a car accident, step off a curb and twist your ankle, have a fight with a friend, or come down with an illness. We don't consciously choose for these experiences to happen, but if we do not pay careful enough attention to what we give our focus to, we let our feelings and emotions run wild. What we experience is the result of what we have thought and felt. Our power always lies in taking control of the present moment.

If we understood the link, we would know that we have to guard our thoughts carefully and give our attention to only what we want, a simple yet difficult outlook for our reality-based society. After all, we have free will, which gives us the power to consciously or unconsciously create our life experiences. *We don't get what we want; we get what we are and what we give out.* I experienced this for myself, and it was not until much later that I really understood how the pieces fit together.

I was in a state of blame over some choices I made as a parent and truly felt terrible over some words that were said. This was brought to my attention, and it hit a place deep inside—a place I could not even speak about. I spent a long time in that place of deep regret and self-blame. Even in comparison to the wonderful things I thought I had done as a parent, I focused only on the negatives and felt deeply remorseful and accountable.

About a year after that, I was diagnosed with thyroid cancer. As a non-smoker living a healthy lifestyle, I was shocked. At the time, I was reading about Louise Hay, a spiritual teacher and author I admire, and how she healed her own cancer. I bought some of her books and CDs. I spent time practicing the meditations, visualizations, and self-reflections. I felt immeasurably better—in perfect health. I requested a second biopsy, and that one came back negative. The doctor who called me said he had no explanation for the discrepancy and gave me the choice to cancel the surgery and follow up with monitoring. I remember that conversation and what I felt. It was like I finally realized a truth I had been searching for. I had an amazing sense of control over my life, and I felt like I truly understood the power of the mind and our beliefs. I was in an incredible place—powerful and peaceful. I told friends and family what I believed to be true and received many doubtful responses, but that was fine because I believed in what was true for me.

Not long after this occurred, I visited my primary doctor who has little belief in the power of the mind and self-healing. His words were harsh and condescending as he asked me what kind of voodoo I thought I was doing. He said there were explanations for the negative biopsy (there are) and that I was foolishly putting my life in danger. I left his office with an oppressive feeling of fear washing over me. Had I really been so self-indulgent and foolish? I thought of all the people I had shared this with. Other doctors and other people in my life had the same reaction; fear and doubt began to wash over me in waves. I felt betrayed by the very beliefs that had given me so much peace. If what I had believed in was really true, how could I still have cancer? If everything happens for a reason, how could I go through the experience of receiving a negative biopsy report, just to have the surgery after all? I could not make sense of any of it.

I chose to have surgery, and when the biopsy turned out to be malignant, I was even more devastated. I felt foolish when I realized I had shared my beliefs with my friends and family; some even had serious medical issues or had lost loved ones to cancer. Although done with pure intention, my observations now sounded pompous and unrealistic. I could not make sense of why this happened and thought it would have served the greater good for others to see we have control over our experiences.

Despite my confusion, I still believed in the process and the possibilities, but I could not make sense of the outcome in my own life until it finally dawned on me. This realization felt like a blanket was finally lifted from over my head. Nothing is done *to* us. Nothing is done *for* us.

It took me a long time to come to a place of clarity about what I believe happened and why it happened. I realized that it wasn't something that happened to me; it was an experience I created, both the positive and the negative. When focusing on feeling perfectly healthy and entertaining only forgiveness, love, and positive thoughts, my cancer resolved and disappeared. Once the fear and worry returned, in my response to the fears of others, it returned again. It was created the first time in response to my persistent feelings of guilt and remorse, which was my system's wake up call, drawing my attention to a way of looking at myself that did not serve me and was not based in truth. Our feelings play an important role for us; they let us know when we are based in illusion and not in love—for others or ourselves.

This experience taught me that nothing is being done *to* us. We do the choosing and orchestrate the events in our lives through our thoughts, belief systems, and our prevailing emotions. My feelings of embarrassment and foolishness were my ego's attempt at keeping me small, not recognizing my power. I have only told a few people how I truly feel about this experience because I choose not to expose myself to the doubts of others. I do not condemn these doubts, and I understand where they come from since I had them myself. I know my family, friends, and doctors only had my best interests in mind, but in all of our experiences, both positive and negative, we have to come to a place where we receive clarity about them. They have to make sense to us and us alone at a very deep level. We need to understand why these experiences occurred, what our lessons were, and what our roles were in them.

Our own truth about these experiences is all that matters. There is a feeling of completeness when we reach that place; it is like fitting the last piece into a jigsaw puzzle. It is a feeling of simplicity and clarity, and when we find it, we finally recognize our own power.

This clarity is priceless and does not require approval from anyone else. It is a peaceful and powerful outlook to live your life from.

• •

Think back to a time of deep emotion for you. Remember the state you were in, and connect those feelings to an event that occurred after that point. Could there be a connection? Could we direct more of our experiences than we believe?

• •

A Belief In Possibility

To believe in things you can see and touch is no belief at all.
But to believe in the unseen is both a triumph and a blessing.

    – Bob Proctor, motivational speaker and life coach

THE BELIEF THAT anything is possible is a precious gift we can give our children. This notion may be viewed as unrealistic and simplistic, but it is a belief that holds much power. We have a choice to believe in our perceived limitations or our own infinite capabilities. We can choose to believe in the finality of constraints or our unlimited potential. How do you want your children to live their lives, and upon what do you want them to base their choices?

We can lead our children to believe they are weighed down by alleged inadequacies or help them to know they are perfect, worthy, and powerful creatures. This outlook will determine the scope of their possibilities and the breadth of their experiences. Envision children who view each day as a gift with limitless possibilities, revel in the sunset or in the beauty of a rainbow, and believe in the wonder of Christmas morning and the power of a wish. Picture a child as he or she experiences the magic of Disney World or witnesses a puppy being born. We can encourage our children to hold onto this pure, unfiltered way of viewing the world as they grow.

This universe holds limitless possibilities if we are open to them, but we can only have what we believe to be true—and what we receive is in direct proportion to the level of conviction we have. Unfortunately, people give up on their dreams very easily because they cannot guarantee that their efforts will result in what they want. Our egos try to shield us from disappointment, but we have a choice to live our lives suffocating under its safety or venturing out to discover what opportunities the world holds for us. Nelson Mandela, South African anti-apartheid revolutionary, politician, and philanthropist said, "There is no passion to be found in settling for a life that is less than the one you are capable of living."

We can choose lives of mediocrity or opportunity. We can demonstrate faith in humankind or focus our attention on the atrocities we hear about. We can revel in the wonders around us or focus on the areas of lack and decide that it is just the way of the world. I do not believe everything in our world is perfect; I am not being naive. However, we can place our focus beyond the surface of the event and look at transcending the experience in search of the treasure it holds.

We may crush our children's dreams (and our own) under the guise of appearing wise about the ways of the world and coming to terms with the reality of a situation. However, we become what we believe, and we receive experiences that are a match to the energy we exude, so it is no surprise when life confirms those limiting beliefs for us. Is it better to be secure in knowing what an outcome will be or to take a chance and envision possibilities that match our dreams?

Parenting choices are often based in fear or disapproval. We fill our children with anxiety and apprehension as we explain the many dangers lurking in the world while we overlook all the wonderful occurrences going on around us. We reward them for being quiet and inconspicuous, for blindly following rules, conforming to the mainstream, and remaining compliant. We teach our children to play it safe in order to avoid disappointment.

If we revisit our approaches and guide our children to view their lives as wonderful adventures filled with joy, growth, and creation, it would lay the groundwork for limitless possibilities. If we filled them with optimism, hope, faith, and confidence while we encouraged them to be unflappable in the pursuit of their dreams, their world would expand—and the universe as a whole would benefit from their contributions.

Help your children have the courage and faith to imagine all of the possibilities life can bring because their experiences will be enriched by this approach.

. . . .

Make a choice to believe in the unseen, the unbelievable, the impossible. Encourage your children to do the same. How do you feel? Silly? Hopeful? Free?

. . . .

The Power Of Love

And in the end, the love you take is equal to the love you make.

—Paul McCartney, English musician,
singer, and songwriter

RESEARCHERS WERE CONDUCTING an experiment in a laboratory at Ohio State University. Investigators were studying the subject of diet-induced atherosclerosis, a disease that is a leading cause of death for Americans. The researchers studied groups of rabbits that were all fed identical high-cholesterol diets. One group had 60 percent less incidence of disease, but the researchers could not determine the reason. They came to discover that the man in charge of this particular control group loved rabbits. He would talk to the rabbits and hold them every day, showering them with love. They determined that this was the only different variable. It resulted in a 60 percent reduction in disease for his control group, proving that *love is powerful medicine.*

Love is a word that is used often, but being in a state of love is not a frivolous place. Love represents joy and beauty, forgiveness and compassion, tolerance and respect. Love takes work, and it takes honesty. Love can be infinitely joyous, but it takes a lot of courage.

We are always either in a state of love or fear. Criticism is fear, judgment is fear, and depression and anger are byproducts of fear. Compassion and kindness are love; forgiveness and patience are love. When we are in a state of love, we look at the world differently. With a higher level of understanding and serenity, our self-centered ego is taken out of the picture and replaced by a universal consciousness. In a state of love, we understand that we are all part of a larger picture and are connected to a greater purpose. We don't focus on the differences between each other; instead, we gravitate toward the commonalities.

Just like the grains of sand on the beach, we are all part of a larger entity. When we realize that we are connected by a universal love that is infinite and pure, we choose to unconditionally love our world, each other, and all the creatures that inhabit our planet. Most importantly, we love ourselves. We have patience for the obstacles, differences, and challenges. We react to situations from a loving perspective where everything seems to make more sense.

Love attracts experiences that are positive, and since we are all energy, a loving perspective and choices based in love create a better life for us. Loving ourselves is the greatest gift we can give to our children because it allows our gifts and talents to emerge unscathed by our own inner critics. We can share these gifts with others and show our children they are free to share their own. Love is why we are here on this planet—to grant love to ourselves and to demonstrate love for others. The love we gave and the love we received is the only thing that remains when we leave.

To discover love, we have to let down the walls to find out that we will do more than survive—we will come through with more strength and compassion for others and ourselves. Only when we let down those walls can we fully experience true joy, forgiveness, and acceptance. What we have experienced before that point is a mere shadow of what could be.

We are afraid this process will break us, but we are stronger than we give ourselves credit for. The journey to self-love means looking at areas of ourselves that we would rather pretend do not exist and viewing them through the lens of understanding and forgiveness. If we deny those areas, hiding from them instead, they gain power over us and direct our lives in ways we do not want. Shining a light of love, forgiveness, and acceptance on those areas helps them dissipate.

This is not always easy because we place conditions upon love for ourselves that we would never demand of others. We concentrate on our flaws and seek only perfection; we don't let ourselves off the hook for much, but being human means encompassing love for ourselves, including our imperfections, and knowing that our truth is that we are perfect just as we are. We can't truly love or forgive others until we bestow this gift upon ourselves. When we accept ourselves, we see the connection to truly loving and accepting others.

Our children need to learn the lessons of self-love, forgiveness, and acceptance. Sometimes it just takes a little faith to view a situation from a different perspective.

Be willing to let go of beliefs that limit you from being the truly amazing, loving, powerful, joy-filled being that you are.

· ·

Where do you put up walls to keep love from entering your life? Why are those walls there? Do they continue to benefit you? Would you fall apart if they were down? Consider that dismantling them could lead to a greater experience of what life could offer.

· ·

Things Change

Life is a series of natural and spontaneous changes. Don't resist them—that only creates sorrow. Let reality be reality. Let things flow naturally forward in whatever way they like.

—Lao Tzu, philosopher

JOHN BRAMBLITT LOST his sight in 2001 after a series of seizures and became angry, withdrawn, and depressed. He could no longer read or write, but he decided to try his hand at painting, which he never had done before. He thought it might help him express all the emotions he was feeling. John said that if the paintings were terrible, he would not have to see them anyway; he had no intention of sharing them with others.

John first coated the canvas with puff paint to form an outline and then chose bold colors to express his emotions. His work is striking and vivid, full of feeling and passion; the reaction to his paintings has been extremely positive. John's work has been featured in a multitude of art galleries, and his paintings are in high demand. John has also received accolades for his YouTube video from 2008. He volunteers to teach art workshops to people and neighborhoods that lack access to art instruction, and he was awarded the US Presidential Award for Volunteerism. John now experiences a profound sense of calmness and purpose, which he did not have before losing his sight.

There will be times in life when you encounter difficulty, ranging from mildly annoying experiences to those you consider devastating. Whether you are five or forty, it always feels like it will be this way forever. If we choose to hold onto those memories and feelings, the power of those feelings will intensify, but they will dissolve if we release them.

Everything changes, and everything evolves; of that, we can be certain. Life is in a constant state of fluidity. Relationships and events we deem momentous in our lives change direction, shape, and evolve. It is important to convey to your children when they are feeling hurt or angry that their feelings will not remain as painful as they are at that moment. There will be difficult days at school, friends will let them down, family members will disappoint them, or they will encounter the loss of someone special. The feelings they experience at first are raw and strong, but they will change with time. Help your children reflect on a time when they experienced a difficult event, and help them remember how those feelings dissipated.

It is important to realize that there is a bigger picture—greater than this challenge we are facing. This experience teaches us something we need for our growth and helps us develop in certain areas. The difficulty level of the experience corresponds to how badly we need to learn the lesson it holds, and it is likely that we ignored easier opportunities to do so in the past. That is difficult to comprehend at the time, but the way you view these challenges will change. Sometimes that is enough to focus on until things get better.

These difficult times also demonstrate what we do not want. These events point us in the direction of what we do want—and they help us define it more clearly. They give us information about how we are viewing life and how we are living it. Sometimes, the pain that these difficult times brings us is what we need to motivate us to make changes. Change is necessary for our growth, and the space this change creates gives us a place for something new. However, we have to make the room for it and give it permission to be there.

Often, there is some message to learn from these difficult events—something we need to acknowledge or work through—despite the fact that it is hard. If we resist them, we intensify their impact on our lives and don't allow any transcendence; we are unable to see the gifts they hold for us. Author and teacher Wayne Dyer said, "You are not stuck where you are unless you decide to be."

I know that my diagnosis of thyroid cancer was difficult for me, and going through the process of dealing with it, emotionally and physically, was not easy. However, because of the experience, there were gifts I would not have recognized otherwise. I was able to look honestly at the parts of myself I was not granting forgiveness to and was able to find a place of understanding and compassion. As a result, I was able to forgive others in my life that I harbored resentment toward. I began the journey of authentic self-expression and received the inspiration to write this book as a result. I was able to gain insight into the direct correlation between what we think, believe, and feel and what we experience in a most profound way. If given a choice now, I would choose to have gone through that experience in order to receive the insight I have gained from it.

An African proverb states, "Smooth seas do not make skillful sailors." There is a reason for everything in our lives; nothing is random. Beneath the most seemingly insignificant experiences are ways to facilitate growth, if we choose to look closely. The obstacles we face provide perfect opportunities for our development.

When your children encounter difficult experiences, try to help them surrender to them. Help them look at the positives, in order to learn something from them. If that does not work, help them accept the events for what they are, considering that later on, they may make some sort of sense.

Keep in mind that life is replete with transformation, and the impact these challenging times have on our lives will change, as everything does.

What difficult experience led to something positive you could not foresee when it occurred? Consider the reasons it happened and how it has shaped your life in some way.

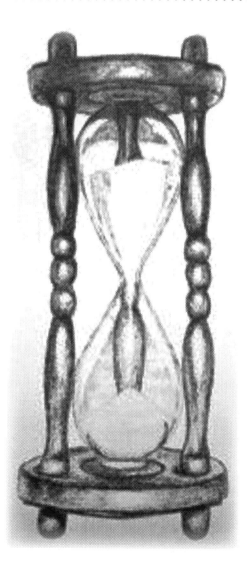

Kids Think They Know Everything

Too many people grow up. That's the real trouble with the world, too many people grow up, they forget. They don't remember what it's like to be twelve years old. They patronize, they treat children as inferiors. Well, I won't do that.

—Walt Disney, American business magnate, film producer, director, animator, and screenwriter

CHILDREN KNOW A lot more than we give them credit for. Adults could learn a thing or two by observing how children interact with the world. As we grow, we become so rational and ambitious that we lose sight of the pleasure in each moment. Children don't hesitate to burst out in a resounding belly laugh when something is funny. They scream at the top of their lungs and throw tantrums when they are angry, and babies let you know exactly what they need in every moment.

What about children's fascination with the beauty of nature and their connection to animals? They know nothing is more important than a warm hug and a sloppy smack on the lips. Children greet each moment with an open heart and a capacity to adapt to the experience at hand. They do not meet every experience with a preset agenda, and they don't take themselves so seriously. Children do not prejudge each other with stereotypical views, and they generally make the best out of each situation.

Children believe in miracles, and they are open to all possibilities, unless we fill them with doubt and fear. Children know how to feel feelings, express them, and let them go unless we teach them it is wrong. They can be angry with a sibling one minute and gleefully conspiring with them the next. They know how to laugh until it hurts and cry like there is no tomorrow. What about their ability to love purely and forgive totally? The pureness in this love can bring you to your knees.

Don't take the joy of living out of your children and replace it with a need to be practical or teach them that they need to be inconspicuous. Don't overreact or judge their feelings harshly, and don't be afraid of their feelings. *Place your attention on what they are doing right, not on what they are doing wrong.*

Take a page from your children's book and live life spontaneously; appreciating the joy in each moment, expressing how you feel, and letting these feelings pass.

Know you are perfect just as you are - just as they are.

. . . .

Look at your children and consider ways you could learn from them. What could our children teach us if we were open to learning from them? This week, decide to approach an experience the way a child would and look at the outcome.

. . . .

Living Real

Our deepest fear is not that we are inadequate. Our deepest fear is that we are powerful beyond measure. It is our light, not our darkness that most frightens us. We ask ourselves, Who am I to be brilliant, gorgeous, talented, fabulous? Actually, who are you not to be? You are a child of God. Your playing small does not serve the world. There is nothing enlightened about shrinking so that other people won't feel insecure around you. We are all meant to shine, as children do. We were born to make manifest the glory of God that is within us. It's not just in some of us; it's in everyone. And as we let our own light shine, we unconsciously give other people permission to do the same. As we are liberated from our own fear, our presence automatically liberates others.

—Marianne Williamson, spiritual teacher and author

IT TAKES COURAGE to live an authentic life—to express what you want, to stand up for your beliefs, and live a life of your choosing. To do otherwise can leave you feeling seriously uninspired. When you are not living in alignment with who you truly are, you feel conflicted and unsettled.

Your truth is something you believe with all of your being, regardless of the truth of others. By honoring this truth, you make choices that resonate with you and which you can stand by with pride. Your truth is something of great importance, and it is something you understand on a very deep level. It may make others uncomfortable, but this does not mean it is wrong or untrue. When a belief is true for you, it does not need the validation of others. That is all that matters.

Getting in touch with my truth began in an unexpected way. I was overweight, breaking out in hives, and newly diagnosed with asthma. I knew that if I did not take control of my health, the future would hold more challenges. The doctors I sought out gave me medication to control the symptoms, but they did not help me discover why I was having them. It was not until I met a doctor who was honest in telling me that he did not know enough about the holistic view of disease, but could recommend a book on the subject for me. The book led me to additional resources and practitioners who viewed the body as a whole organism; they practiced functional medicine and holistic treatment. Sixty pounds lighter, the symptoms were gone—and I felt better than ever before. Stepping through this doorway led me to open my mind in other areas, and when my friend suggested I read a spiritually-based book that explained how we create our own reality, I jumped in with both feet and my newly opened mind.

Embracing a spiritual journey has not been without its challenges and doubts. I have been on the receiving end of much good-natured teasing and raised eyebrows from friends and family. However, it feels true to me, which is all that really matters.

I have met so many people who are searching for something more—more meaning, satisfaction, and fulfillment in their lives. Instead, they seem to be experiencing more angst, anxiety, and stress in everyday living. They have a pervasive feeling of emptiness and a desire to understand the reason for it all. At some point, they wonder if this is all there is. A spiritual outlook has alleviated some of this for me, but like everything else, it is a work-in-progress. Learning this information has opened up a new mode of viewing the world in a way that that makes more sense and offers me deeper meaning for my experiences. It has made me feel powerful and inspired, centered and grounded. Writing this book is part of my process as well—embracing my self-expression, sharing what I believe in, and hoping it can be of service to others.

The practice of living real, of being who you are, and living your truth is an important practice to teach your children. Our society as a whole does not encourage this practice, particularly for children. They are encouraged to keep their thoughts private as if others' feelings are more important than their own. They have been taught to be quiet at the expense of their own feelings. American author and radio personality Garrison Keillor said, referring to children, "You have taught me to be nice, so nice that I am full of niceness, I have no sense of right and wrong, no outrage, no passion."

Our children have become used to a certain level of complacency, often backing away from taking a stand or speaking up for what they believe in. They are told to keep their heads down and to not make waves. This approach, while often easier, does not lead to decisions they are always proud of.

We have to teach our children to be true to themselves first—or their lives will never work. Give them permission to let individuals and situations go if they do not reflect who they are. Sometimes this is painful to admit, but it is more painful in the long run to continue in situations that are not authentic.

Demonstrate this practice with your children by the way you live your life and by examples of your own authenticity. You can show them the importance of this by standing behind what you believe and by matching your actions to your words. You can display this by not sacrificing your core values and beliefs in order for others to be happy, including your own parents. It is cathartic to express your voice and outlook on topics you have once expended energy to repress. Show your children that it is important to remain true to their own beliefs, even when it is unpleasant for others. Once you practice the art of being true to who you are, your example gives others encouragement to do the same.

It takes a secure parent to empower your children in this way. When you let your children discover what is true for them, it will create strong, secure, courageous, and emotionally healthy individuals.

Those children will grow to be the leaders who have the vision and fortitude to transform humanity in ways our world so desperately needs.

• •

Where in your life are you not living real? What area needs examining and reevaluating? Do you have the courage to do so, or do you prefer the safety that your choices currently offer? Make a list of what might occur if you made a new choice. Are you ready for the consequences of a new decision?

• •

Acceptance

When I let go of what I am, I become what I might be.

—Lao Tzu, Chinese philosopher, founder of Taoism

I HAVE ALWAYS considered myself an open-minded, tolerant individual. I would disagree whenever that perception was challenged, but I should have realized that something you have to defend is something worth examining.

I have come to realize that, often quite unknowingly; I have judged the choices and actions of others. When we judge others, we are in a negative place. What we criticize in others is often a part of ourselves that we have difficulty accepting, and the negativity, anger, and faultfinding are always directed back toward us. When we have no need to blame or find fault with another, it is because their actions do not hit a nerve. Our judgment, even if unspoken, does neither party any good. When I find myself in this place, I ask myself if I want be happy or right. And believe it or not, you don't have to be right to be happy. No one has to change for you to be happy; however, needing to be right places the power of how you feel in another's hands.

Negativity alters the energy of a relationship, and when we judge others, we are really judging ourselves. Anyone who has looked on decisions in the past with regret knows how critical this judge and jury can be. We need to consider this feeling of blame and look at the role it plays in our lives. Why do we steadfastly hold on to it, and how can we let it go? One way to release this is by acknowledging that what we focus our attention on increases, and it serves us to focus on the aspects of our children and our lives that we find pleasant. We are always affecting the energy of our relationships, and this is one of the most powerful ways to do so. Visualizing the types of family atmospheres and relationships that make us happy is one strategy. Identifying the aspects currently in your family that match this and appreciating them is another.

An additional way to let this judgment go is to have love and acceptance for ourselves. We find it easier to let others off the hook while holding ourselves hostage with unjust declarations and unforgiveness, not realizing they are inexplicably connected. To truly forgive others means we have to give ourselves the same gift. Choosing to let go may mean we find ourselves in unchartered territory of unconditional love. If we have never ventured there, it may be more frightening than not being loved at all.

Radical acceptance of others and ourselves results in our freedom, and it enables us to focus on our own path while surrounding our children with healthy, unconditional love.

. . . .

Write down five areas in your relationship with your children that could use more acceptance. What do you feel when you consider acceptance of these areas? How could acceptance change your view of your role? Your view of your child?

. . . .

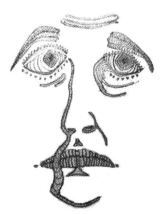

Nature

A three-year-old child is a being who gets almost as much fun out of a fifty-six-dollar set of swings as it does out of finding a small green worm.

—Bill Vaughn, American columnist and author

HAVE YOU EVER noticed that children are happiest when they are in nature? Take them to a park or the seaside, and they will amuse themselves for hours, reveling in the natural beauty surrounding them. Nature is here for us to enjoy, no matter where we live or what our finances are. We can visit a park in the city to surround ourselves with greenery or visit our local seashore for a stroll on the beach. We can take a drive down a country lane to enjoy the meadow or look at the majestic mountains in the distance. We can even go to our own backyard or patio and enjoy the sunshine and the garden. Just breathing in the fresh air revives us like no store-bought luxury can. The energy found in our natural environment gives us more vitality than we get from stopping into Starbucks any day.

Every part of nature is a wondrous occurrence, from cracks of thunder or blades of grass swaying in a gentle breeze to soothing drops of rain on a windowpane. Think about the aspects of nature that you and your children gravitate to. Is it the roar of the ocean, the ripples of a lake, snow-covered mountains, or the solitude of the forest? For me, it is the seashore where my senses are enveloped by the smell of the salt air, warm sun on my skin, hot sand between my toes, and cool water on my skin. I feel as if I can let everything go, and I am truly at peace.

Everyone has a special place in nature that revitalizes them. Khalil Gibran, Lebanese artist, poet, and writer said, "Forget not that the earth delights to feel your bare feet and the winds long to play with your hair." We are connected to nature on a very deep level, and when we give our children the gift of spending time appreciating its beauty, they become energized, grounded, and inspired. Teach your children to protect and conserve the resources of the universe that they so enjoy. It is our responsibility to give as well as to enjoy.

Despite your busy lifestyle, make time to enjoy our wonderful earth in whatever setting appeals to you, and give your children unscheduled time in nature. It is time worth spent on every occasion.

Obligations and responsibilities will be there when we return, but we return with more stamina to handle them and are able to keep them in perspective.

* *

Make a plan to spend time this week in your favorite part of nature. Give your children the same gift. Consider the ramifications of this choice. How did you feel during and after? Does this experience change your perspective on daily life? On choices that you make regarding your time?

* *

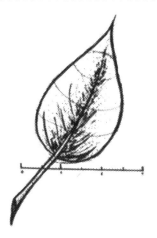

Career

Your work is to discover your work and then with all your heart to give yourself to it.

—Buddha, sage and founder of Buddhism

THE PURPOSE OF a career is to find something that brings you joy and fulfillment while providing a service to the world. If we tell our children that they must find a career that leads to financial wealth first and foremost, we point them in the direction of seeking something that may not make them happy. I often cringe when a student shares a passion for something, and the parent says, "You will never make any money doing that." Looking at the student is like watching a balloon deflate. I understand the reason for the statement, but there is little truth to it.

There are many individuals employed in careers that are not associated with a lucrative salary, but they are very prosperous and happy. Do you want your children to work at a job that they dread going to every day, but they put up with it because they are making a lot of money? Is this the life we envision for our children under the guise of needing security—or do we want more for them?

I heard a statement once that has remained with me ever since: *You can only have what you believe to be true.* If we believe in our dreams, and ourselves, they will come to fruition. The road to this place does not always occur in a straight and steady direction though. There may be bumps in the road and lessons to be learned, and these lessons would not have come without the challenges.

We have to let our children navigate this path on their own, in their own way, even when it is difficult for them—and for us to watch. This does not mean that we can't lend a hand when it is needed, but we should not be directing the process. There are many successful, wealthy individuals who are living lives of purpose and fulfillment who would not be in the place they are now without going through difficulties. And many happy and fulfilled individuals are not wealthy but would not change a thing in their lives.

We all have talents that can provide a much-needed service to the world. The automobile mechanic who repairs cars so people can drive safely is performing a service. The financial planner who helps elderly people live an independent lifestyle supports others. A funeral director who brings comfort during a difficult time makes a significant contribution. The key is loving what you do and doing it with love. Writer Joseph Campbell said, "Follow your bliss and the universe will open doors where there were only walls." If we demonstrate more faith and require less assurance about the outcome of following our hearts, we will be pleasantly surprised.

Too many people put time and energy into careers that are unfulfilling and detrimental to their health. They look back after a lifetime of complaining and wonder why they did not take the risk to try something else. That "something else" connects with our hearts and souls if we take time to listen and move past the fear. American entrepreneur Steve Jobs said, "The only way to do great work is to love what you do. If you haven't found it yet, keep looking. Don't settle. As with all matters of the heart, you'll know it when you find it."

We are not defined by the successes of our children—and neither are they. We are wonderful, complete beings, and we are perfect with or without successful careers.

Give your children permission to find what inspires them.

Encourage your children to find out what makes their hearts sing and their souls sigh with happiness.

. . . .

Where do your children find their joy? What about you? Decide to incorporate more of these experiences into your daily lives.

. . . .

Gratitude

Everything is perfect in the Universe—even your desire to improve it.

—Wayne Dyer, American self-help
author and motivational speaker

Nick Vujicic was born with no arms or legs. If you have the opportunity to hear him speak, it is worth your time. Nick embraces all of the experiences in life that he can with an open heart and a courageous spirit. He can be seen golfing, surfing, playing the drums, and giving inspirational talks at corporations, schools, and congregations. Nick expresses gratitude to God for giving him the opportunity to serve as his minister. He teaches that if you fail, you can always try again; in the end, it only matters how you finish. Nick keeps a pair of shoes in his closet because he believes in miracles.

Some days, it seems hard to feel grateful for your life. You look at others and envy their circumstances while you focus upon what you don't have. Reaching for a feeling of gratitude is a matter of perspective, and when we change our perspectives, everything changes.

There are many things in our lives that create dissonance for us. We have a house, but it's not the one we want. We have clothes to wear, but they're not the latest styles. We have friends, but not the satisfying relationships we wish for. Our health may be good, but it's not great. The key to feeling grateful begins with truly appreciating what we *do* have. Changing our focus to the aspects of our lives that we appreciate changes the energy we emit. This energy is responsible for bringing us experiences that match it, a concept that is both simplistic and complex.

It is important to teach our children that their present states of being create their futures, and gratitude is the key to attaining what they want. If we focus on moments in the past that we don't like, we are creating identical futures. Consequently, expressing true gratitude for what we have is the elixir for what ails us. We can acknowledge gratitude for those in our lives even if they do not always act as we want them to. We can be grateful for our health, knowing that someone else may face more difficult issues. We can be thankful for the money we have, knowing many individuals have much less.

Gratitude is a very powerful place, and it can be the starting point for better experiences to come. This place can serve as a bridge to connect us with even more positive feelings in our lives; gratitude is the passageway for a miracle. Help your children recognize the power this state of being holds for them; it can help them propel their lives in the directions they want to go.

We get what we are, and if we focus upon what we are lacking, we will get more of the same. When we are in a negative place, we say to the universe that we want more experiences to match that state because we are defining who we are by our outlooks. When we focus upon what we are thankful for, that list will grow. When we tell the universe we are healthy, prosperous, loved, and happy, we get more of the same.

Make a list of all the things you are grateful for; you may be surprised at what you see. Start with everyday miracles: the opportunity to experience another day, a beautiful sunrise, the changing of the seasons, a child's smile, a warm blanket, the unconditional love of a pet, a home-cooked meal, gazing at the stars, or the chance to tell someone you love them. Every day brings opportunities to feel gratitude if we look at our lives with open hearts.

Sincere gratitude—consisting of our thoughts, words,

feelings, and beliefs—allows the universe to connect us with more experiences that match this feeling.

· ·

Make a list of all the things you are grateful for, both big and small. Experience a feeling of gratitude as you get in touch with just how fortunate you really are. Encourage your children to complete the same exercise. Keep the lists that you created in a place where you will see them and where they can remind you of all your blessings.

Try this exercise: Every day, you and your children will write something down that you are grateful for and collect them in a box or container. Read through all of your blessings together every month and at the end of the year.

· ·

Parenting Our Parents

How far you go in life depends on your being tender with the young, compassionate with the aged, sympathetic with the striving, and tolerant of the weak and strong. Because someday in your life you will have been all of these.

—George Washington Carver, American scientist, botanist, educator, and inventor

ACCORDING TO US Census projections, there are almost six million Americans age eighty-five or over today, and by 2040, the number is projected to be more than fourteen million. These days, people are living longer, but not necessarily better. Medical interventions, gadgets, and myriad medications are enabling seniors to live lengthier lives, but not always with the quality they want or with the resources to take care of themselves.

Many people find themselves responsible for taking care of their parents while caring for their children. This may come at a period of their lives when they thought they would have time for themselves. This situation is challenging for both parties, and it takes many people by surprise. Even when we notice our parents aging and having more difficulty with everyday tasks, denial lets us think they can handle it as they have handled other matters in their lives.

It's hard when we see our aging parents struggling or needing more of our help every day. It is difficult for our parents to be at the mercy of others more often and to be less able to make decisions for themselves. When we take over the responsibilities for our parents' safety and welfare, we experience a multitude of emotions, ranging from anger, worry, fear, and loss. None of these are wrong, and we should not judge ourselves for having any or all of those feelings.

When I began to experience this situation with my mother as her dementia worsened and her physical abilities declined, I railed against the role I knew I would need to assume. I was angry, resentful, and scared about all that she was going through and what was to come for her. I worried about how I would assume all the responsibilities this role would entail. The more I resisted what was happening, the worse I felt. When I let go and surrendered to the experience, enjoying my mother's company with no preconceived notions and knowing I would handle what life would bring, I no longer felt burdened. Love is what always remains. Maybe it will be in a different form or have new rituals, but if you want to find it, you will.

There is a lot of dysfunction within families, and sometimes it is hard to be in a place where you take over this new role without feeling resentful. We need to remember that our parents could only give us what they had themselves. They gave us what they were capable of giving, and they did their best. At times, it was great, and other times, it was lacking. In those times particularly, we may have to look for a place of acceptance and forgiveness in our relationships with our parents to help them when they need us and to move on from the past.

This experience gives us an opportunity to rise to a higher level, to make decisions with integrity, and to enjoy the present moment. We might decide we need to slow down a little and recognize what really matters. We may learn to be less selfish and more patient, to be generous with our time, and to accept the frailties of life with the gifts it offers. We can show our children that people are not expendable, and we can give our children the gift of helping to care for their grandparents.

All our experiences are defined by our perceptions of them, and this one is no different. We define who we are every day—not just in the grand moments but also in the quiet ones when no one is looking.

· ·

Spend quality time this week with your parents. Take time to tell them why you love them or what you appreciate about them, even if you have had a difficult relationship. If your parents have passed, recall some special memories, and spend a few moments telling them how you feel about them.

· ·

Words Matter

The way we communicate with others and with ourselves ultimately determines the quality of our lives.

—Anthony Robbins, American life coach, self-help author, and motivational speaker

THE ABILITY TO communicate effectively is at the heart of all healthy relationships. Nowhere is this more important than between parent and child. Harmony and productive co-creation occurs when we feel understood, when our needs are met, and when we are able to express how we feel. When we are angry or resentful, it is generally because some type of miscommunication occurred—and we don't understand the other person's point of view.

Throughout history, words have been used to incite riots, start wars, facilitate genocide, and initiate hate crimes. However, they have also been used to mend broken hearts, create peace between warring nations, and inspire people to make choices with integrity. The words you speak to your children are of no less importance. They are a predictor of how the next generation of children will live. Our children will live with love, confidence, and faith in their hearts or with fear, resentment, and anger.

Communication is paramount in our relationship with our children. We need to tell them how we feel, answer their questions, and listen to their feelings. We need to communicate authentically; this means being vulnerable enough to tell them how we really feel and what is important to us. We need to recognize the power of our words, to understand they have the capacity to heal or to wound. We need to remember that, sometimes, we should think before we speak. Our words should tell our children that they are wonderful, capable, and brilliant— not because of something they did, but just because of who they are. Our words should be honest, loving, full of encouragement, and kind. Our words should contain our truth instead of our fears.

Our words are important. We need to choose them with care because they shape our children's spirits. Every word we speak comes from an act of love or it doesn't—every word, every time. We can speak our truth with kindness, our guidance can come free of our own agenda, we can request respect with respectful words, and we can share our feelings with authenticity. We can use our words to offer apologies to our children when we make mistakes or help our children see difficult situations from new perspectives. Our words can empower our children or crush them. Once spoken, you can't take them back; you can only apologize for them and begin again. Author Peggy O'Mara said, "The way that we talk to our children becomes their inner voice."

Listening is an important form of communication: hearing our children's concerns, answering their questions honestly, and giving them space to express their feelings. We need to listen to the meaning behind their words, give them time to tell us what they need, watch their body language, and try to decipher what is really going on. Sometimes we forget that part because we are so concerned about having them listen to us, understand us, or benefit from what we have experienced. But it is a two-way street, and if you do all the talking, they will tune you out eventually.

It is important to have a good line of communication established before your children reach adolescence because topics become more involved, and there is much they need to know. Communication takes various forms. You can express what you need, and the importance of this should not be underrated. You can also do something meaningful for your child, plan to spend time together in their favorite places, or cook their favorite meals.

You can give them hugs when they are feeling down or just hold them when they are little.

My husband recently wrote each of us a letter, telling us things he felt unable to express verbally, but he very much wanted to share them. He was very funny—mailing it to each of us—so he couldn't change his mind. I love that letter; it means a lot to me, and I look at it often. Even though the words were not spoken, they mean just as much.

It is essential to communicate with your loved ones and to say things you want others to know, whether it is to a child, parent, spouse, or friend. Tell the people you care about how you feel, why you do what you do, what your worries are, what your gripes are, and most importantly, how you feel about them. Clear up misunderstandings, explain your actions, clear the air, and share your thoughts.

Often, one of our biggest regrets in life is not telling those we love how much they mean to us and not recognizing that we only have this moment to do so.

• •

Take time this week to tell those you love how you feel about them. Think of what your heart wants them to know, and take the time to tell them before your mind has the chance to talk you out of it.

• •

Your Inner Child

It's never too late to have a happy childhood.

—Tim Robbins, American actor, screenwriter, director, producer, musician, and activist

THERE IS ANOTHER child who needs your love and attention. Your inner child is the one who resides within your heart and looks to you, and only you, to care for them. This one you have forgotten from so long ago now needs your recognition, compassion, and attention. We all have this child living within us, and while the concept may sound strange, there is much to discover if we take some time to get in touch with this child.

Our inner child holds all of our painful experiences and raw feelings from the past because they don't know how to let go of them or how to transcend them. They are stuck holding onto coping methods that may have served you in the past but stand in the way of your greatness now. This child needs you to get in touch with this place inside of you in order to move on. When your inner child moves on, you can move forward in your life too.

You may have been the child who was always told you never did anything right, the one who was punished for making a mistake, or the one who was never the favorite. You may have been the one who was only safe when you were invisible or the one who was told you should be seen and not heard. Maybe you were the one who was only recognized for your achievements, the one who had to keep family secrets, or the one who knew you had to seal your heart to protect its vulnerability. If we listen carefully to what our inner child needs, we find ways to improve the current state of our lives. We heal old wounds and let go of patterns that do not serve us now. We have to be willing to let go of these dysfunctional patterns to improve our lives, even though their predictability provides comfort. This child is counting on you because you are their only salvation.

Our inner child can lead us to discover treasures that were hidden away when we were told to be inconspicuous and responsible. We can help them experience now what they could not when they were young. We need to get in touch with this child and give them permission to let go of self-blame, feelings of not being enough, or the fear of abandonment. Only we can help them release painful experiences and transcend old hurts and digressions. As they evolve, our lives transform.

Our inner child has much they want to teach us; they have pearls of wisdom to share with us. They tell us not to be so much of an "adult" and to live as children do, carefree and adventurous. They want us to take advantage of the opportunities that life gives: to take a risk, take a chance, be bold, be outrageous, say how you feel, not take things so seriously, and to always be open to love. They show us that nothing is more important than doing what makes you happy, what inspires you, what makes you feel alive. They beg us not to give up on our dreams and to move past our fears. They tell us that love is the only thing that matters and that we can choose love in every interaction we have, no matter how insignificant.

Our inner child is inviting us to enjoy life, to draw and paint, sing and make music, to express our creativity. To swim, go on roller coasters, let ice cream drip down our chins, make sandcastles, and dance in the rain with them. They want us to go outside and gaze at the stars, watch sunsets, hug a tree, and jump in puddles. They tell us not to be afraid to cry like a baby and to laugh out loud.

Your inner child will jump up and down with glee as you do

these things, and you will know that it is so because you will feel an incredible level of freedom, joy, and exhilaration.

As you heal this child, you will heal yourself.

• •

Find a quiet place. Focus on your heart space, and ask your inner child what they want and what they need. Be still and listen to the response. Write down the answers you receive, and resolve to give your time and attention to them.

• •

Use the space below to write your own message to your child—from your heart to theirs:

_____

_____

_____

_____

_____

_____

_____

_____

_____

_____

_____

_____

_____

_____

_____

_____

_____

Resources

Below, you will find recommended resources. Many of these teachers and authors offer a wide array of books, DVDs, CDs, workshops, and online programs.

Self-Growth, Spirituality, and Wellness

Beth Miller:

Free Guided Meditations
www.bethmillermeditations.com

Louise Hay:

You Can Heal Your Life
Heal Your Body: The Mental Causes for Physical Illnesses and the Metaphysical Way to Overcome Them
Modern Day Miracles: Miraculous Moments and Extraordinary Stories
You Can Create an Exceptional Life (Louise Hay and Cheryl Richardson)
All is Well: Heal Your Body with Medicine, Affirmations, and Intuition (Louise Hay and Mona Lisa Schulz)
You Can Heal Your Heart: Finding Peace After a Breakup, Divorce, or Death (Louise Hay and David Kessler)
Cancer (CD)
www.louisehay.com

Neale Donald Walsch:

Conversations with God
The Only Thing That Matters
When Everything Changes, Change Everything
Happier Than God
www.nealedonaldwalsch.com

Marianne Williamson:

A Return to Love
A Course in Weight Loss
The Law of Divine Compensation: On Work, Money, and Miracles
The Age of Miracles: Embracing the New Midlife
www.marianne.com

Susan Shumsky:

Divine Revelation
Miracle Prayer: Nine Steps to Creating Prayers That Get Results
The Power of Chakras: Unlock Your 7 Energy Centers For Healing, Happiness, and Transformation
How to Hear the Voice of God
Exploring Meditation: Master the Ancient Art of Relaxation and Enlightenment
www.divinerevelation.org

Christiane Northrup:

Women's Bodies, Women's Wisdom: Creating Physical and Emotional Health and Healing
Mother-Daughter Wisdom
The Power of Joy
www.drnorthrup.com

Lissa Rankin:

Mind Over Medicine: Scientific Proof That You Can Heal Yourself
www.lissarankin.com

Wayne Dyer:

I Can See Clearly Now
Wishes Fulfilled: Mastering the Art of Manifesting
Excuses Begone: How to Change Lifelong, Self-Defeating Thinking Habits
Ten Secrets for Success and Inner Peace
Getting in the Gap
www.drwaynedyer.com

Sonia Choquette:

Grace, Guidance, and Gifts—Sacred Blessings to Light Your Way
Ask Your Guides—Connecting to Your Divine Support System
www.soniachoquette.com

Deepak Chopra:

Creating Health: How to Wake Up the Body's Intelligence
Self-Power: Spiritual Solutions to Life's Greatest Challenges
The Shadow Effect
Creating Affluence: Consciousness in the Field of All Possibilities
www.deepakchopra.com

Esther and Jerry Hicks:

The Law of Attraction: The Basics of the Teachings of Abraham
Ask and It Is Given
The Amazing Power of Deliberate Intent: Living the Art of Allowing

Money and the Law of Attraction
www.abraham-hicks.com

Pam Grout:

E-Squared: Nine Do-It-Yourself Energy Experiments That Prove Your Thoughts Create Your Reality
www.pamgrout.com

Deborah King:

Truth Heals: What You Hide Can Hurt You
Entangled in Darkness: Seeking the Light
www.deborahkingcenter.com

Foundation for Inner Peace:

A Course in Miracles
www.acim.com

Rhonda Byrne:

The Secret
The Power
The Magic
Free download on this website:
The Science of Getting Rich by Wallace D. Wattles
The Master Key System by Charles F. Haanel
www.thesecret.tv

Joel Siegel:

Lessons for Dylan: From Father to Son

Brad E. Sachs:

The Good Enough Teen: Raising Adolescents with Love and Acceptance (Despite How Impossible They Can Be)
www.bradsachs.com

Zoe Weil:

Above All, Be Kind: Raising a Humane Child in Challenging Times

Philip Permutt:

The Crystal Healer
www.thecrystalhealer.co.uk

Gary Kraftsow:

Yoga For Wellness
www.viniyoga.com

Shambhala Classics/Chip Hartranft:

The Yoga-Sutra of Patanjali
www.shambhala.com

Ilchi Lee:

Healing Chakras: Awaken Your Body's Energy System for Complete Health, Happiness, and Peace
www.ilchi.com

Health and Nutrition

Jennifer Kelly:

The Healthy Kitchen 101
www.feedingyourlife.com

Mark Hyman:

UltraPrevention—The 6-Week Plan That Will Make You Healthy for Life
The UltraMind Solution: The Simple Way to Defeat Depression, Overcome Anxiety, and Sharpen Your Mind
The Blood Sugar Solution: Turn the Tables on Diabesity
UltraMetabolism: The Simple Plan for Automatic Weight Loss
www.drhyman.com

Mehmet Oz:

You: On a Diet
You: The Owner's Manual
You: Staying Young
You: Raising Your Child
www.doctoroz.com

David Wolfe:

Superfoods: The Food and Medicine of the Future
Longevity Now: A Comprehensive Approach to Health Hormones, Detoxification, Sugar Immunity, Reversing Calcification, and Total Rejuvenation
Eating for Beauty
www.davidwolfe.com

Andrew Weil:

8 Weeks to Optimum Health: A Proven Program for Taking Full Advantage of Your Body's Natural Healing Power
Spontaneous Healing: How to Discover and Embrace Your Body's Natural Ability to Maintain and Heal Itself
Healthy Aging: A Lifelong Guide to Your Well-Being
www.drweil.com

George Mateljan:

The World's Healthiest Foods: Essential Guide for the Healthiest Way of Eating
www.whfoods.com

William Davis:

Wheat Belly: Lose the Wheat, Lose the Weight, and Find Your Path Back to Health
www.wheatbellyblog.com

Children's Books

Rich Specht:

A Little Rees Specht Cultivates Kindness (First Ride Publishing)
www.reesspechtlife.com

Deepak Chopra:

On My Way to a Happy Life
Teens Ask Deepak: All the Right Questions
You with the Stars in Your Eyes

Christiane Northrup:

Beautiful Girl: Celebrating the Wonders of Your Body

Louise Hay:

I Think, I Am: Teaching Kids the Power of Affirmations
The Adventures of Lulu

Neale Donald Walsch:

Santa's God: A Children's Fable about the Biggest Question Ever

Wayne Dyer:

I AM: Why Two Little Words Mean So Much
Its Not What You've Got: Lessons for Kids on Money and Abundance
Goodbye Bumps: Talking to What's Bugging You (Wayne Dyer and Sage Dyer)

Esther and Jerry Hicks:

The Sara Series
A New Adventure

About The Author

COMBINING THE EXPERIENCE of raising two daughters and extensive practice in the field of counseling with young adults and their families, Jeanmarie Wilson was inspired to write a book for parents connecting practical guidelines for raising children with spiritual ideology.

Jeanmarie has a master's degree in School Counseling from Long Island University and has been a school counselor in the New York State public school system for more than twenty years. She is also the co-founder of a college consulting company, *Your Journey To College*.

Jeanmarie has two rescue dogs and helps support animal rescue—a cause that is very important to her. Influencers along her spiritual journey include Esther and Jerry Hicks, Marianne Williamson, Louise Hay, and Neale Donald Walsch, as well as many others listed at the end of the book. She enjoys yoga and meditation, cooking healthy food, gardening, swimming, hiking with her husband and dogs, and spending time at the beach.

Jeanmarie lives on Long Island in New York with her husband.